The Parent's Guide to SEND

T0385402

of related interest

The Parent's Guide to Specific Learning Difficulties
Information, Advice and Practical Tips
Veronica Bidwell
ISBN 978 1 78592 040 0
eISBN 978 1 78450 308 6

Parenting Dual Exceptional Children
Supporting a Child who Has High Learning Potential and
Special Educational Needs and Disabilities
Denise Yates
Forewords by Sal McKeown and Lydia Niomi Christie
Illustrated by Paul Pickford
ISBN 978 1 78775 810 0
eISBN 978 1 78775 811 7

Parenting a Dyslexic Child
Edited by Gillian Ashley
Foreword by Gavin Reid
ISBN 978 1 78775 426 3
eISBN 978 1 78775 427 0

Championing Your Autistic Teen at Secondary School
Getting the Best from Mainstream Settings
Debby Elley and Gareth D. Morewood
Foreword by Peter Vermeulen
ISBN 978 1 83997 074 0
eISBN 978 1 83997 075 7

A Different Way to Learn
Neurodiversity and Self-Directed Education
Naomi Fisher
Illustrated by Eliza Fricker
ISBN 978 1 83997 363 5
eISBN 978 1 83997 364 2

The Parent's Guide to SEND

Supporting Your Child with Additional Needs at Home, School and Beyond

Gary Aubin and Stephen Hull

Foreword by Andy Kirkpatrick

Jessica Kingsley Publishers
London and Philadelphia

First published in Great Britain in 2025 by Jessica Kingsley Publishers
An imprint of John Murray Press

2

Copyright © Gary Aubin and Stephen Hull 2025

The right of Gary Aubin and Stephen Hull to be identified as the Author of the Work has been asserted by them in accordance with the Copyright, Designs and Patents Act 1988.

Foreword Copyright © Andy Kirkpatrick 2025

Widgit Symbols © Widgit Software Ltd 2002-2024 www.widgit.com

Number of pupils with an EHC plan or SEN Support, by type of need, 2022/23 on page 56, used under Open Government license v3 www.nationalarchives.gov.uk/doc/open-government-licence/version/3

Percentage of pupils with a statement or EHC plan by type of provision, England, 2015–2023 table on page 57, used under Open Government license v3 www.nationalarchives.gov.uk/doc/open-government-licence/version/3

SEND Code of Practice 9.44 Request Assessment from local authority diagram on page 77, used under Open Government license v3: www.nationalarchives.gov.uk/doc/open-government-licence/version/3

A CIP catalogue record for this title is available from the British Library and the Library of Congress

ISBN 978 1 80501 045 6
eISBN 978 1 80501 046 3

Printed and bound in Great Britain by Clays Ltd

Jessica Kingsley Publishers' policy is to use papers that are natural, renewable and recyclable products and made from wood grown in sustainable forests. The logging and manufacturing processes are expected to conform to the environmental regulations of the country of origin.

Jessica Kingsley Publishers
Carmelite House
50 Victoria Embankment
London EC4Y 0DZ

www.jkp.com

John Murray Press
Part of Hodder & Stoughton Ltd
An Hachette Company

The authorised representative in the EEA is Hachette Ireland,
8 Castlecourt Centre, Dublin 15, D15 XTP3, Ireland (email: info@hbgi.ie)

This book is dedicated to all the hardworking families, educators, carers and others doing their best for our young people. Thank you!

Contents

Foreword by Andy Kirkpatrick **11**

Acknowledgements **14**

Preface **15**

Introduction **16**
The shape of the book   16
For you, our readers   17
Terms we use in this book   18

1. **Definitions, Diagnoses and the Education System** **19**
Defining SEND   19
When you notice something is different   25
Common diagnoses   26
Anxiety disorders   27
Attention deficit hyperactivity disorder   29
Autism   30
Down's syndrome   34
Dyscalculia   36
Dyslexia   37
Dyspraxia (developmental coordination disorder – DCD)   41
Hearing impairment   43
Moderate learning difficulties   44
Oppositional defiant disorder   46
Pathological demand avoidance   47
Physical disability   49

Speech, language and communication needs 50

Tourette's syndrome 51

Visual impairment 53

2. **Schools and the Education System** **55**

The national context 56

The government's response 60

How schools support children with SEND 63

Support in exams 70

The legal framework for support 71

The legal duties to parents 73

Education, Health and Care Plans 74

Choosing a school 85

Finding out about local schools 89

Legal rights around school choice 96

Annual reviews 99

Transition points 101

Transitioning to higher education 104

Funding for pupils with SEND 104

Attendance to school 105

Addressing difficulties your child is having at school 106

School trips 114

Life in secondary school 117

Life after secondary school 120

The world of work 121

3. **Supporting Your Child's Learning** **124**

Using visuals 124

Forward- and backward-chaining 140

Praising your child 142

Building resilience in your child 142

Motivating your child 144

Helping your child to stay in one chair 145

Developing writing 147

Developing reading 150

Studying at home 156

4. Life at Home **160**

Sleep — 160

Toileting and self-care — 163

Clothing — 166

Dressing — 167

Eating — 168

Bilingual and multilingual families — 171

Travel and outings — 173

Siblings and other family members — 178

Special occasions — 181

SEND merchandize — 182

Routine — 183

Encouraging communication — 186

Promoting independence — 188

Challenging behaviour — 189

5. Supplementary Therapies **193**

Early intervention? — 193

Applied Behavioural Analysis — 195

Art therapy — 197

Animal-assisted therapy — 198

Music therapy — 199

Occupational therapy — 201

Rebound therapy — 202

Speech and language therapy — 203

Talking therapies — 204

Accessing therapy — 207

6. Support for Parents and Siblings **208**

Claiming Disability Living Allowance — 210

Claiming Carer's Allowance — 211

Claiming other benefits as a young person with SEND — 212

Support with housing — 212

Sources of information and advice — 214

Books relating to SEND — 215

Social media — 218

A Note Before We Leave You **221**

Glossary **222**

References **225**

Bibliography **230**

Appendix **232**

Foreword

Climber Andy Kirkpatrick (1971–) is one of the UK's most accomplished mountaineers, having pioneered numerous daring solo ascents of long and strenuous climbs around the world. In addition to his achievements in the hills, Andy is a successful public speaker and award-winning author, having won the prestigious Boardman Tasker Prize for Mountain Literature for both his first and second books.

My mum first realized I was different when my baby brother was born. She began to see how he hit all the developmental markers much quicker than me: crawling, walking, speaking, reading, writing, tying shoelaces, getting a job, learning to drive and getting a better job with a pension.

Knowing no better, and being a very content baby, then child, then adult, I didn't pay much attention to being 'slow' or 'lazy' or my lack of focus and attention until the age of six, when my inability to tie my shoelaces resulted in a pair of state-of-the-art Velcro shoes from Woolworths. Then, I realized I was not the same as everyone else. I was not a lace-tier, a reader, a writer, a teacher concentrator. I was something else. Something that didn't quite fit.

Later on, these negative labels were rebranded to the more sympathetic sounding 'learning difficulties', 'special needs' or some ill and continually redefined 'disorder', and with them, 'special lessons' about cats and mats and bats. Nevertheless, on leaving school, I still had an elementary-level reading and writing age and the concentration of a four-year-old.

I was 19 and on the dole when I had my first test for dyslexia, primarily as a way to game the system and so be able to sign on without being badgered by 'the man'. But the test was an eye-opener: I got 15% on the numeracy paper and 99% for spatial awareness, which showed that something was up with my brain. The outcome was the realization I needed to avoid the world of abstraction, numbers, memory and things inside my head, and stick to the analogue world of physical reality and things.

So I decided to become a professional mountaineer.

Of course, with no graduate programme, internships or fast-tracking into this field, this was a long and steep career path. The process to relative success took about 30 years. Mastering the craft of mountains, faces and big walls was also very dangerous. Still, beyond memorizing the heights, the odd compass bearing or the phone number of the mountain rescue, it did avoid many of the corrupted parts of my brain. Yes, it was perilous, and I nearly died several times, but with limited choices, and no need for a written test, it was all there was.

Then a strange thing happened. There's not a lot of money in climbing mountains no one has heard of, but there is a little to be made in writing about such things. And so, just like tackling a mile-high piece of vertical granite, I took my primary school writing skills and tried to apply them to real-world experience in order to share my stories.

The first thing I wrote, on an early second-hand home computer (running Windows 3.0), took two solid years of work before it was in any fit state to publish. Luckily, I lost the floppy disk (or deleted that document by accident several times), so I had to start again, and again, and again. But, like climbing that mountain, I had no other option but to keep trying; after all, what else could I do?

And so, with my words hammered, shaped and refined innumerable times, along with my misshapen brain, I finally faxed (yes, pre-internet) my story to the US magazine *Climbing*, the most prestigious climbing magazine in the world. The following day, I got a fax saying they loved it; and just like that, this remedial kid became a writer.

Half a life later, I have more books with my name on than I can keep track of, not only in English but in French, German, Italian, Spanish, Polish, Russian and even Korean. I've picked up many awards – somehow – for the things I have written, and most remarkable of all, my entire income comes from the books I now publish myself; odd, when you consider that becoming a writer was the worst career choice I could ever have made (apart from lace-tying instructor or accountant).

How did this come about? It was partly about understanding the value of my uniqueness – or weaknesses – and then exploiting the advantages and disadvantages it brought. But, to be honest, I don't know what it proves. Except perhaps that how I was assessed to be did not define what I achieved and how I went about it. I was lucky to be free: free to make my own choices and mistakes; free to fail and to succeed; and free to turn the world of mountain literature on its head. Yes, my brain might not be 50% yin and 50% yang like most people, but look what a brain can do with 99% yin and 15% yang!* I was also born stubborn, or stubbornness was born in me.

As a final note, it was when I had my own kids that I really understood how lucky I had been to be born into a world in which I was viewed as just 'slow'; for all the cruelty of that, the opposite is perhaps worse. The opposite can be a world in which a child is only understood by the label they have rather than the person they are. My advice would be to understand the difference, but don't let it define everything. You're reading this book because of something unique in your child. Make him or her know themselves for who they really are. Your job is to help them to shine, however that may look for them.

Andy Kirkpatrick

---

*   Joke

Acknowledgements

We would like to thank Jessica Kingsley Publishers for seeing the potential in this book and for their support throughout the process.

We particularly need to thank every parent or carer who has supported this book in some way. Many of the most poignant and useful words in this book have been written directly by the parents of children and young people with a special educational need or disability (SEND) and can be found in personal accounts that feature in every section. Many other parents have supported us, not by writing for the book but by making sure we understand what content they would find useful in a book like this.

The expert colleagues at the Independent Provider of Special Education Advice (IPSEA) have been as insightful as ever as they helped us to ensure we were always interpreting correctly the often-complex law in relation to SEND.

We also need to thank our families – Emily, George and Nancy; and Vicci, Sam and Lewis – for their support, patience and love while we put this book together.

Preface

We (your humble authors) met in our first year of university, thrown together in a student flat with seven other strangers. A friendship quickly developed that lasted through university, into the world of finding jobs in our 20s and beyond into family life.

A naive early ambition to open a series of schools around the world turned out to be unrealistic (for many reasons). Our journeys into education continued though, with Gary training to be a teacher and Stephen working in global education for the British Council, both in the UK and in Latin America.

Gary's career soon went in the direction of SEND, with him becoming a secondary special educational needs and disabilities coordinator (SENDCO) before beginning to work across schools and for a range of organizations in relation to SEND.

Stephen developed his own understanding of SEND through taking on a chair of governors role for a special school (as if by fate, before the birth of his autistic son).

This professional angle should come across strongly throughout the book. Our ability to understand effective school leadership, to navigate local authority processes and to develop effective classroom practices stands us in good stead for writing a book such as this.

This book would be incomplete, however, without Stephen's experience of raising his son, who was born in 2016. Whether in terms of initially accepting your child's differences, building routines into the home environment or choosing to select a special school for your child, Stephen's personal experience will shine a light on the journey many of you may be embarking upon.

INTRODUCTION

There are some wonderful books out there for parents. Many of them have helped us in our own journeys within SEND.

We've never found one, however, that does quite what we've tried to do here. We wanted to better support families to navigate the world in relation to SEND, whether their child is at home, at school or in their community.

We wanted to offer one book that tells families about the benefits they might be eligible for, the local authority services that might support them and the clinicians they might speak to along the way.

We wanted to offer one book that suggests how you might embed a successful morning routine, develop your child's communication skills or help them manage toileting independently.

We wanted to offer one book that shares how schools might adapt their classroom environments, approach school trips or deploy a teaching assistant to support your child.

This merging of professional and personal experience is what makes this book unique. We have also chosen to include numerous stories and case studies from other professionals and parents. These illustrate the varied viewpoints and intricacies of the world of SEND from others who also have invaluable first-hand experience.

The shape of the book

We begin the book by providing an introduction to SEND. We look broadly at what constitutes a SEND, describing how differences in children are understood conceptually in England. We provide insights into 15 of the most common types of SEND, focusing particularly on how each need is currently defined, what an assessment pathway looks like in each case and what support a school might provide.

Next is a chapter all about the school system – how it works and how to work with it. We help you to consider which school might be right for your child; we help you to know what it's reasonable for any school to provide. We take you through the ways additional support can be funded, and the role parents play in this. We look at what parents might do if and when difficulties arise.

Following that, we look at how you might support your child's learning at home. We share ideas and resources that might support your child to develop as a reader, writer and resilient learner.

We then delve into how you might support other areas of your child's development and wellbeing at home – from sleeping to eating. We provide ideas to help your child to self-regulate, approaches that promote independence and thoughts on how to approach special occasions.

There's a chapter all about therapies, which can become an overwhelming part of family life in some cases. For a range of common therapeutic approaches, we tell you what they are, what they set out to do and how they might be accessed.

We follow this with a chapter on support for families. We take you through some of the main benefits you might be eligible for and suggest further sources of information to support you on your journey through SEND.

One book can only go into so much detail about everything from blue parking badges to fussy eaters. And so we tell you, in every section, where you can go for more information and support. We wanted to write a book that supports parents to thrive in the SEND world, so we've included various, 'What should I ask...?' questions to help you navigate discussions with a range of professionals.

For you, our readers

This book is primarily written from the English context and as such is informed by up-to-date policy and practice within this area, but we are confident that much of the information will also be useful to those in other parts of the UK.[1] It is written primarily with parents of

---

1   Policy making in education (and various aspects of health and social policy) is devolved in England, Northern Ireland, Scotland and Wales.

younger children in mind, who are perhaps just starting out on their own journey within SEND. But there are insights and sections that will be handy for parents with older children too, including when your child with SEND is entering adulthood.

It will also be useful to other family members, carers or family friends involved in a child's life and education. Support professionals may also find it helpful. It may be read as a whole or section by section, depending on what is most useful to you.

Whatever your position, whatever your reason for picking up this book, we hope that you find something useful in it. Just as all children with SEND are unique, your experience of parenting a child with SEND will likewise be unique to you. Enjoy the ride, and enjoy being a parent!

Terms we use in this book

Accepted terms within SEND are not universal. We have attempted to use the terms recommended by NHS England in the 'Making information and the words we use accessible' document published on its website (NHS England, n.d.). This includes using identity-first language where it is specifically recommended (e.g., 'autistic child', 'disabled pupil'). In cases where it is not specifically recommended, we have used person-first language (e.g., 'children with SEND', 'pupils with an EHCP'). We acknowledge that there is not a universal agreement on these terms, that language use is contested within SEND and that preferred terms evolve over time.

Where the term 'parents' is used in this book, we use it to refer to the child's parent/legal guardian.

Finally, we have tried to strike a balance in terms of considering SEND as a 'difficulty' or a 'difference'. Often things *are* difficult for many children with SEND and it would be wrong for us to underplay or not acknowledge these difficulties. That said, the difference in the way the child experiences the world is not a within-child deficit – it is often about the way the world needs to operate so that their gifts can be valued and their potential fulfilled.

CHAPTER 1

DEFINITIONS, DIAGNOSES AND THE EDUCATION SYSTEM

In this chapter, we're focusing on supporting your working understanding of SEND. Parents shouldn't feel that they need to become medical experts (your expertise lies in your knowledge of and love for your child), but a basic level of knowledge around SEND makes it easier to contribute to the discussion and should therefore be empowering for families.

We'll help to explain how SEND is defined in England by introducing some common concepts and hearing directly from some children and adults who themselves have SEND. We'll take you through some of the predominant types of SEND, including how a diagnosis is made, what support a school might give and where parents might look for further support or information.

Defining SEND

It's perhaps worth starting with the question, 'What is SEND?' The legal definitions of SEND exist in the Children and Families Act (2014):

A child or young person has special educational needs if he or she has a learning difficulty or disability which calls for special educational provision to be made for him or her.

A child of compulsory school age or a young person has a learning difficulty or disability if he or she:

1. has a significantly greater difficulty in learning than the majority of others of the same age, or
2. has a disability which prevents or hinders him or her from making use of the facilities of a kind generally provided for others of the same age in mainstream schools or mainstream post-16 institutions.

Children and Families Act, 2014, Part 3, 20 (1-2)

The SEND Code of Practice published in 2015 (Department for Education and Department of Health and Social Care, 2015) gives a bit more detail to schools. It clarifies that the definition of 'disabled' in this context is broader than some may think:

Many children and young people who have SEN may have a disability under the Equality Act 2010 – that is '...a physical or mental impairment which has a long-term and substantial adverse effect on their ability to carry out normal day-to-day activities'. This definition provides a relatively low threshold and includes more children than many realise: 'long-term' is defined as 'a year or more' and 'substantial' is defined as 'more than minor or trivial'.

While this may be a broad definition, it doesn't mean that every difficulty in school equates to SEND. It doesn't mean that every time a school intervenes or provides additional support, it requires placement of the child on their 'SEND register' (see glossary). Nor does it mean that every child who finds their learning difficult has a SEN. As a parent, it's important to note that your child may receive additional support of some kind without ever needing to go near a SEND register.

Slow progress and low attainment do not necessarily mean that a child has SEN and should not automatically lead to a pupil being recorded as having SEN.

SEND Code of Practice (2015)

'Labelling' children

Any discussion about special educational needs (SEN) must reiterate – and hold in mind – the fact that diagnoses and labels are just linguistic tools to help us to identify and address individuals' strengths and challenges in relation to the definitions above. They should never lead us away from the fact that every child should be viewed and treated as intrinsically valuable for being exactly who they are.

Whether we like them or not, however, labels are often necessary for health and education authorities to assess children, organize the kind of support they need and train teachers and therapists. But research into, and knowledge of, diagnosable conditions themselves tells you very little about any individual. Good teachers will educate the individual first and foremost and will use specialist knowledge and practical interventions they have gained to help along the way.

BEING AUTISTIC AND 11 YEARS OLD – WHAT IT MEANS TO ME

Barney tells us what being autistic means to him.

What are you really good at?

Video games, cycling, word searches and expressing my emotions.

Describe some of the teachers you've had.

My worst teacher was very strict and got cross very quickly, for example, I would miss out some full stops in most of my sentences and she would say, 'No no no, you're doing it all wrong.'

The best teacher I had was quite kind and kept her patience a lot. She was quite helpful with making you feel a bit better about things, for example, if I was feeling really upset because I couldn't do maths or something, she would explain it to me in a useful way.

What does being autistic mean to you?

Being autistic means I have a disability, sort of, it just means my brain is different from other people's.

In life, I feel like it both helps me and it cannot help me. Ways it helps me are that I am good at seeing patterns and that makes me good at chess. I don't know if this is part of autism but when I listen to my audiobooks, I calm down quickly.

I do get overwhelmed with lots of noise, which is weird because I can make a lot of noise myself! I get overwhelmed in busy places, but I'm not sure exactly what it is that I don't like about them. I do know that I am different, but not massively, and I think being different makes you special.

Everyone has a personality and mine is just a bit different. It's not that I'm weird or a freak; everyone is different (and anyway, I don't really care if I am weird – it's fun being weird if you have someone to do it with!).

Can you tell me one or two things that your parents do that really help you?
Fidgets really help me a lot. I have an old phone on which I listen to audiobooks and this makes me feel more independent, confident and responsible. My parents give me squeezies (squeezing arm/hand massage) at bedtime, which helps me to relax. My parents are awesome.

Barney, aged 11

Identifying SEND is complex
Identification and labelling of special needs is not an exact science. Clearly, it is easier in some cases than in others. For example, it is quite straightforward to identify a child with sight in only one eye. It is much more complex and difficult – and indeed contentious – to assess and separate pupils and to assign them a diagnosis of, for example, 'learning difficulties', rather than simply embracing the natural range of aptitudes present across a population.

This becomes even more complex when assessing, against 'age-related expectations', those pupils who are in the same year group as others but were born in the summer, almost a year after the oldest of their peers. These pupils are at a clear disadvantage compared with older children, who have had much more time to learn and experience the world.

Furthermore, some disabilities can be overcome by making adaptations to the environment. For example, to be diagnosed with autism you must have difficulties with social communication. But in the right environment or with certain people, an autistic person might not display any problems whatsoever in communicating or interacting. And thoughtful building design can mean mobility differences may cease to be problematic.

There is also a wide degree of crossover, or co-occurrence, in SEN. For example, autistic people can develop anxiety disorders because of sustained trouble understanding and predicting the social world. Some children have two or more diagnoses that are not related, and this can be tricky to unpick, especially in young children because they are developing so much anyway.

Remember, the most important thing in school is that your child is supported to get the most out of their learning experiences, not necessarily whether or not they've been diagnosed. A lack of appropriate services and/or long waiting times often means schools have to identify and support needs, irrespective of diagnostic labels.

Putting a ceiling on expectations

Having a diagnosis may be a mixed blessing: on the one hand, it can be helpful (or even necessary) to access the support you need; on the other hand, there is a risk your child may be prejudged.

There is research evidence demonstrating how labels can predetermine pupil attainment. In one classic study, Rosenthal and Jacobson (1966) chose children at random from across the attainment range and labelled them 'bloomers'. Teachers were told the bloomers had potential for excellent academic achievement. When IQ tests were readministered months later, the bloomers had made significantly higher IQ gains than the children who had not been singled out as bloomers. The researchers concluded that if you tell a teacher a child is able, they will teach them as if they are able and the child will make more progress.

The danger is that this principle could be applied inversely for children with SEND; i.e., beliefs about a pupil's limited abilities will result in people lowering their expectations of what is possible. Good teachers will be mindful of this effect and will ensure all children reach their academic and social potential.

It carries the weight you give it

Outcomes should not be predetermined by the labels children carry and the related assumptions we all have about them. You may find yourself frequently challenging others' assumptions about your child. Indeed, your own assumptions may be challenged, and this can be an empowering and positive thing. The foreword to this book includes a real-life example of this, in which Andy Kirkpatrick – who is severely dyslexic – became an award-winning author.

A PARENT'S VIEW – THRIVING AT SCHOOL WITH SEND

Charlene shares her early journey within SEND – full of praise for the support her son has received and full of love for the boy he has become.

I am the proud mother of a lovely 12-year-old boy diagnosed with global delay, a learning disability and autism.

He was diagnosed very early, at two years old. It was quite clear he was autistic before he was diagnosed, as he made no eye contact, didn't respond to his name, lacked speech and had a range of restrictive and repetitive behaviours.

Entering the education system

As a child, my son received a nurturing and inclusive experience alongside both neurodivergent and neurotypical children,[1] giving him a space to play and be part of the world while benefiting from the smaller class and less stimulating environment when he needed it.

If I could offer any advice to parents of a child in early years (three to five years), I would say to place your child with professionals who understand the complex and basic needs of your child, enabling tailored strategies to develop your child's unique sensory profile.

As a parent, my child's specialist nursery was a godsend. They helped me to understand more about his diagnosis and how to manage his behaviours, but also to consider my own wellbeing. They gave me tools I still use to this day. A setting that considers both the children's and parents' wellbeing is the best thing you could choose for the early chapters of your special journey.

---

1   Neurotypical and neurodivergent are both defined in the glossary.

Starting primary school

He potty trained at five and went on to an amazing special primary school. He again found himself amongst a team of fantastic staff and peers, whom he formed friendships with (and he even fell in and out of love with a girlfriend!). Despite being non-verbal up to the age of nine, my autistic son had a love of language without words and found a way of expressing and reciprocating age-appropriate affection – including towards his special young lady!

Admired and adored

Excellent to know, isn't it. I never thought he would be so admired and adored by the world – the story I had been fed for years was that autistic people are lonely, don't make friends and can't cope in the environment around them. Here was my son with healthy relationships and thriving.

The primary years were fantastic. I saw him challenged and celebrated as he grew in skill, awareness and understanding. Whether with or without words, the primary years helped him to find his voice.

This period really taught me a lot about my son. The thing that changed the perception of our journey was looking at him beyond his autism. Who is he? What does he want? What would he decide if I didn't intervene all of the time? Am I giving him enough pieces to make his own beautiful mosaic called his 'own life'? I had to make space to allow him to have the opportunity to make his own decisions.

When you notice something is different

For every parent, the journey towards their child being identified (and in some cases, diagnosed) as having SEND is unique.

For some, it will be a slow and drawn-out process, while for others, it will feel like the child's SEND label happens overnight.

For some, it will be totally unforeseen, while others will have known something was different for a long time.

Some will struggle to accept that their child has differences that might affect them in the long term, while for others, it will feel like a positive first step to accessing support and making progress.

Parents of children with SEND need to be kind to themselves. Some parents describe the process of identification/diagnosis as one of grief

– grief for the idea of their child sailing through life. For more on how parents might support themselves through the process, see Chapter 6, 'Support for Parents and Siblings', on page 208.

While every journey is indeed unique, the flowchart below tries (as best as possible) to suggest a process for parents to follow when they notice something different about their child's learning:

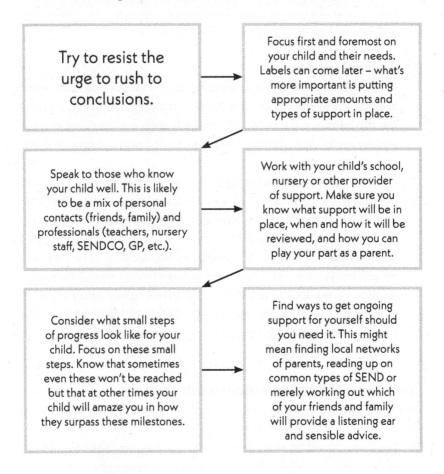

Try to resist the urge to rush to conclusions.

Focus first and foremost on your child and their needs. Labels can come later – what's more important is putting appropriate amounts and types of support in place.

Speak to those who know your child well. This is likely to be a mix of personal contacts (friends, family) and professionals (teachers, nursery staff, SENDCO, GP, etc.).

Work with your child's school, nursery or other provider of support. Make sure you know what support will be in place, when and how it will be reviewed, and how you can play your part as a parent.

Consider what small steps of progress look like for your child. Focus on these small steps. Know that sometimes even these won't be reached but that at other times your child will amaze you in how they surpass these milestones.

Find ways to get ongoing support for yourself should you need it. This might mean finding local networks of parents, reading up on common types of SEND or merely working out which of your friends and family will provide a listening ear and sensible advice.

Common diagnoses

The following list is far from comprehensive and cannot capture the rich diversity of all children; however, it covers many of the most common definitions and diagnoses used in schools today. It includes what are called 'specific learning difficulties' such as dyslexia and dyscalculia, which relate to a specific area of learning. There are also learning difficulties or differences that are broader in nature and relate to learning and development as a whole. There are physical disabilities and there are psychological or emotional difficulties, such as anxiety.

Many of the terms used here intentionally align with the labels used by schools when recording SEND on their SEND register. This does not mean they are the only terms used, but they should support you as a parent to share a common language around SEND with your child's school.

For each diagnosis, we give you a brief overview of what the need or difference is, describing its presentation or talking in diagnostic terms as relevant to each type of need.

We then share what routes to diagnosis look like, including what you as a parent might do if you're trying to access a diagnostic assessment for your child.

We look next at the kind of support that your child might receive in school when they have this particular need or difference. We've tried to include examples of adaptations a teacher might make, interventions that someone (a teaching assistant (TA), the SENDCO) might deliver and support your child might receive in examinations.

Finally, we have tried to steer you towards further sources of support, with weblinks and QR codes to make this as easy as possible for you.

Anxiety disorders

Anxiety is a broad term describing a feeling of stress, panic or fear that can affect everyday life both physically and psychologically. There are currently 11 separate anxiety disorders listed in the DSM-5 (see glossary), ranging from phobias to selective mutism. The most common include generalized anxiety disorder, which is characterized by disproportionate worry about everyday challenges, and social anxiety, which relates to intense fear of social situations.

While we know that anxiety is a normal and healthy human emotion, the DSM-5 describes anxiety as a problem when it is excessive, pervasive and challenging to manage. The NHS website (2023a) talks of children potentially needing professional help when their anxiety, 'affects their behaviour and thoughts every day, interfering with their school, home and social life'.

Diagnosis

Diagnosis of a mental health need such as this will often begin with your GP, though your school could (with your permission) make a referral directly to your local Children and Young People's Mental Health Service (CYPMHS) clinic (see page 207), where a psychiatrist may lead a process of assessment that results in a diagnosis of an anxiety-related condition.

Help that your child may receive at school

A teacher may well embed routines that help to calm a child's anxiety. This will be underpinned by a secure and trusted relationship in which your child knows they are valued and able to succeed.

In relation to learning, your child's teacher might try to remove the unpredictable aspects of the classroom experience for the child – perhaps by embedding consistent routines, by ensuring the child knows what is happening 'now' and 'next', by giving them advance warning before asking them to answer a question aloud and by creating a culture in which making mistakes is an important and valuable step in the learning process.

Outside the classroom, depending on your child's age and current abilities, your school may develop your child's emotional literacy so they can better understand their own feelings. They might develop your child's peer network or, in rarer cases, refer to a therapy service of some kind (see Chapter 5 for common types of therapy used with children and young people).

Potential exam access arrangements may include a 'prompter' (someone to support focus and attention), withdrawal to a smaller room (to remove potential anxiety about being in the exam room with other pupils) and/or supervised rest breaks (the child can come out of the exam for a break without losing any exam time).

Further support
Go to your health visitor or GP
Talk to your child's teacher or SENDCO

Place2Be – mental health support for parents
www.place2be.org.uk/our-services/parents-and-carers

Anna Freud Centre – advice and guidance for parents carers
www.annafreud.org/resources/family-wellbeing

Attention deficit hyperactivity disorder

The first clinical description using the term 'attention deficit disorder (ADD) with or without hyperactivity' appeared in the DSM-III, the American diagnostic manual, in the 1980s (Lange *et al.*, 2010).

The NHS describes attention deficit hyperactivity disorder (ADHD) in children as being diagnosed when the following is present: 'To be diagnosed with ADHD, your child must have 6 or more symptoms of inattentiveness, or 6 or more symptoms of hyperactivity and impulsiveness' (NHS, 2021a).

It's clear from these criteria that not all hyperactive children will have ADHD; likewise, the cause of a child's inattentiveness in class could be a number of things that aren't ADHD (lack of engagement, finding the work too difficult, etc.).

Nevertheless, the National Institute for Health and Care Excellence (NICE) estimates that 3–4% of the population have ADHD (NICE, 2023), with the percentage currently higher in children than in adults (ADHD UK, 2022).

Diagnosis

If you think your child has ADHD, the NHS advises you to discuss it with your child's GP or teacher (NHS, 2021a). Your GP may ask you what your child's school or nursery say; they may even ask for a report or letter confirming the child's difficulties with attention, impulsiveness and hyperactivity in school.

If the GP agrees that assessment is appropriate, they will refer your child to an appropriate professional; this is likely to be a child psychiatrist or paediatrician.

Help that your child may receive at school

Your child may benefit from a range of types of support – some delivered within the classroom and some through out-of-class intervention.

As children with ADHD will often struggle with their focus and attention, teachers may 'check in' on them more often. This might involve more frequently 'prompting' the child, perhaps to turn their focus to the front of the class or to the written task at hand.

They will probably think carefully about where the child is in the class, aiming to place them next to a peer who finds it easier to attend to the teacher and sitting them away from highly distracting areas of the classroom (e.g., next to doors and windows).

Teachers might support a child's focus by encouraging a clear desk so they only have out the items they need. They might additionally support the child to focus on their learning through having shorter and timed tasks, perhaps broken up with 'movement breaks'.

Potential exam access arrangements may include a 'prompter' (someone to support focus and attention), withdrawal to a smaller room (to lessen the impact on other pupils if your child is fidgety or distracted, as well as to support your own child's focus) and/or supervised rest breaks (the child can come out of the exam for a break without losing any exam time).

Further support
Go to your health visitor or GP
Talk to your child's teacher or SENDCO
ADHD Foundation www.adhdfoundation.org.uk
ADHD UK www.adhduk.co.uk

Autism

The National Autistic Society (2023a) describes autism as, 'a lifelong developmental disability which affects how people communicate and interact with the world'. It is a spectrum condition that affects individuals in different ways. It was first identified as a condition in the 1940s, but since then understanding of autism has developed and been refined. Public awareness and understanding of autism has not always been good (or, for that matter, accurate) but it has improved, helped in part by a vibrant community of self-advocates and people such as Chris Packham discussing their lives publicly.

Studies show that 1–2% of people are autistic (National Autistic Society, 2023b), meaning there are around 700,000 autistic adults and children in the UK. Like everybody, autistic people have strengths and challenges, but they tend to share challenges in some of the same areas, including:

- social communication and social interaction
- repetitive and restrictive behaviour
- over- or under-sensitivity to light, sound, taste or touch
- highly focussed interests or hobbies
- extreme anxiety
- meltdowns and shutdowns.

National Autistic Society (2023a)

Characteristics of autism may originate because of differences in the way the brain processes information coming from the senses. The exact cause of autism (if there is one) is not clear; there is no medical test for it, but it sometimes runs in families. The criteria for a diagnosis of autism are refined periodically and currently centre around the first two items in the list above. Labels such as 'classic autism' and Asperger's also come and go, and for this reason, they are sometimes used differently by the scientific and medical communities and by autistic people themselves.

It's worth noting that the emphasis on 'deficits', 'impairments' or 'challenges' is not universally accepted. Some autistic people and those who know them prefer to see autism as a different – and not better or worse – way to be. Terms such as 'neurodivergent' (and the contrasting term 'neurotypical') are now in common use and help to reflect this change in emphasis. It is common to use the term 'autistic spectrum *condition*' instead of 'autism spectrum *disorder*'.

Diagnosis

Diagnosis is made by a medical team with input from a range of other disciplines, such as teachers, educational psychologists and occupational therapists. There are different ways a diagnosis can come about, but in children it generally begins through a school, a GP referral or a referral from another professional such as a speech and language therapist (SALT).

A PARENT'S VIEW – OUR PATHWAY TO DIAGNOSIS
This parent describes the ins and outs of the various stages involved in actually getting a formal diagnosis by engaging with local services.

Our son didn't start using any words at age one or two when most children start talking. This was the first of the 'early signs of autism' that we ticked confidently. Looking back, there were other signs, but we usually played them down – not because we were against having an autistic child; more because he was our first child and we weren't actively looking for signs, nor would we have known if they were present. Absence of speech is pretty clear though and it was at this point we started to ask around for advice – first to a speech charity called I CAN (now called Speech and Language UK: https://speechandlanguage.org.uk) and second to a speech therapist drop-in session at our nearby local authority Children's Centre.

To be honest, most of the advice didn't help because it centred on the assumption that our child wasn't speaking because we weren't providing a rich enough environment for him. I lost count of the number of times I was asked if the TV was always on at home or if we regularly spoke or read to him.

Beginning the process of assessment
After a few meetings at the Children's Centre, we were referred to the community paediatrics team who made some preliminary assessments in a short consultation. The next stage was to attend a series of parent–child sessions with a speech therapist, designed to identify ways we could communicate more effectively with our son. These sessions were pretty patronizing. We had to watch videos of ourselves and comment on what we could be doing better. After this came group 'speech therapy' sessions run by the local authority. I don't think these helped our son to speak or even to communicate any better, but they

did serve as a means to collect material in advance of his diagnostic interview.[2] He also had his hearing checked.

An autism pathway

About a year after his first referral, all the signs pointed towards autism and his communication and behaviour differences started to make much more sense. Around this time, his diagnostic interview was scheduled. There were reports from his nursery and speech therapy and lots of open questions for us on the day.

At the end of it all, it did feel like we'd had to jump through a lot of hoops at first, but we understand the importance of ruling out other reasons for differences in development. Our son was diagnosed aged three-and-a-half years, and although not perfect, the whole process from referral to diagnosis was handled pretty well by our local authority teams and in enough time for us to get an Education, Health and Care Plan (EHCP) (see page 74) before he started school.

Help that your child may receive at school

Many autistic children thrive in mainstream schools with the right support, while special school placements are better for some autistic children. However, the right schools – and indeed the support they offer – will be as varied as the autistic individuals themselves (see page 85 for a discussion on how to choose a school). The support provided to autistic children might focus on communication and understanding and social skills. For example, your child may have their own visual timetable (see page 129) and may need adaptations to help them to understand tasks and routines.

The expectations of how your child completes tasks might look a little different. For example, your child may be given additional time and space; they may be given movement and/or sensory breaks.

The support given while your child is completing a task might also look a little different. They may have support from a teaching assistant. They may have extra support to work with others in groups. The school may also have supplementary provisions, such as lunch clubs, to help to give structure to typically unstructured times of the day.

---

2 'Diagnostic interview' is a term used to describe a consultation, normally with a doctor, in which a series of questions are used to establish if a diagnosis should be made or not.

Good schools, whether mainstream or special, educate all their staff and pupils about autism.

In the English school system, 56% of autistic children have an EHCP (National Statistics, 2023a); the remaining 44% will receive support at the 'SEN Support' level, without an EHCP (see page 74).

Potential exam access arrangements may include a 'prompter' (someone to support focus and attention or to move a child onto the next question), withdrawal to a smaller room (to remove potential anxiety about being in the exam room with other pupils) and/or supervised rest breaks (the child can come out of the exam for a break without losing any exam time).

Further support

Go to your health visitor or GP

Talk to your child's teacher or SENDCO

National Autistic Society
www.autism.org.uk

NHS
www.nhs.uk/conditions/autism

Down's syndrome

A child has Down's syndrome when they are born with a full or partial copy of chromosome 21 because of a change in the sperm or egg prior to birth. This alteration in the genetic pattern is what causes the characteristics of Down's syndrome. Although there have always been people with Down's syndrome, it was first described as a unique set of characteristics in 1866 by a British doctor called John Langdon Down.

A child with Down's syndrome should have regular health check-ups. People with Down's syndrome are more likely to have difficulties with language, vision and hearing. They may need help to develop fine and gross motor skills. They might be slower to process verbal information and need help with social communication. Many also have heart conditions, which are checked after birth.

Those with Down's syndrome have learning disabilities, which can vary in severity. Some children need little additional support at home and at school. Others require ongoing support into adulthood. It is not possible to predict the kind of support children with Down's syndrome will need when they are very young; however, they will likely benefit from more deliberate teaching, including using visuals (see page 124), and respond well to predictable routines and clear use of language.

Some children with Down's syndrome go to mainstream schools, while many go to special schools. You will need to decide what is the best option for your child in the context of your 'Local Offer' (see page 89). Most children with Down's syndrome have an EHCP (see page 74).

Diagnosis

A diagnosis of Down's syndrome is usually made with a chromosomal test after birth.

All expectant parents are offered non-invasive screening tests during pregnancy, but these alone only indicate the approximate likelihood of a baby having Down's syndrome. If screening tests indicate a higher likelihood, parents may have another screening test. They are also offered invasive prenatal (before birth) diagnostic tests, but these tests increase the risk of miscarriage.

Help that your child may receive at school

Teachers may support your child's understanding by using visuals to convey instructions and routines. Information and lessons will often be provided in smaller chunks to lessen the requirements placed on short-term memory. Visual and hearing impairments should be catered for as set out by relevant specialists in these areas.

Children with Down's syndrome may require support to maintain successful peer relationships (though many will not). They will typically receive support with their communication, perhaps through receiving speech and language therapy (see page 203). Communication for children with Down's syndrome may include signing (Makaton) and electronic devices with specialist software, sometimes called 'Augmentative and Alternative Communication' (AAC) devices.

Potential exam access arrangements may include 25–50% extra time, a reader/computer reader (to read the exam questions aloud), someone to scribe for your child and/or a 'prompter' (someone to support focus and attention).

Further support
Go to your health visitor or GP
Talk to your child's teacher or SENDCO
Down's Syndrome Association www.downs-syndrome.org.uk
Mencap www.mencap.org.uk
Contact www.contact.org.uk

Dyscalculia

The British Dyslexia Association (2023a) says that dyscalculia is 'a specific and persistent difficulty in understanding numbers which can lead to a diverse range of difficulties with mathematics'. Like dyslexia, it is known as a specific learning difficulty because it relates solely to difficulties with numbers, such as ordering, number sense and magnitude comparison. Dyscalculia is diagnosed when somebody has particularly severe difficulties with numbers relative to their age and level of education. It is thought to affect about 6% of people (*ibid*.).

Traumatic experiences (inside or outside the classroom) – which is more common in people with dyscalculia – can lead to a condition known as maths anxiety, in which maths-related trauma resurfaces again and again. This can further affect how much somebody is able to learn because of a resultant unwillingness to make mistakes and attempt to learn new skills (*ibid*.).

Diagnosis

Formal assessments for dyscalculia are only available privately. Various screening tools – which indicate tendencies but do not diagnose – are available to schools and other practitioners, however, and these can help teachers and other professionals to identify how best to support your child.

Help that your child may receive at school

Your child should be supported closely to ensure that anxiety around maths does not translate into reluctance to engage in maths. Teachers should be understanding of your child's need to work at a reasonable pace and repeat and practise what is perceived to be 'basic' maths for their age. Tangible materials and visual aids should be used to support conceptual understanding. The reasons for using mathematical functions should be clear.

Potential exam access arrangements may include extra time of 25% or withdrawal to a smaller room (to remove potential anxiety about difficulties the child experiences in maths).

Further support

Talk to your child's teacher or SENDCO

The Dyscalculia Information Centre
www.dyscalculia.me.uk

British Dyslexia Association
www.bdadyslexia.org.uk

Dyslexia

Dyslexia is a learning difficulty that primarily affects the skills involved in accurate and fluent word-reading and spelling. It is thought to affect these skills because of differences in the way information is processed by dyslexic people's brains.

Like autism, dyslexia is not universally thought of as a negative and deficit-defined condition. Rather, it can be seen as a neurological difference to which there are positives as well as negatives. For example, dyslexic people may have strong reasoning skills and be particularly visual and creative. Unfortunately, however, many dyslexic people find education difficult because of its emphasis on reading and writing, memory and cognition. Your child's experience may depend in large part on how well the school is able to identify and support challenges as they arise.

The exact cause of dyslexia is unknown, but it does tend to run in families. Its prevalence is not known for sure, but in the UK, it is thought to affect 10% of the population (British Dyslexia Association, 2023b).

Diagnosis

Formal assessments for dyslexia are not widely available on the NHS and cost around £500 privately. Various screening tools – which indicate dyslexic tendencies but do not diagnose – are often available to schools and other practitioners. These can help teachers and other professionals to identify how best to support your child.

Help that your child may receive at school

Teachers may well provide additional support for writing and reading tasks and for tasks that require significant planning and sequencing. For example, they may support pupils with how to structure longer writing pieces. They may give advance warning and support to prepare for reading aloud. Your child may be provided with alternative means to communicate, such as a computer/tablet and dictation software. Good teachers will value the content of work separately from a pupil's ability to spell consistently or read quickly.

Though less supported by strong academic evidence (if it works for your child, does it matter?), some schools will provide coloured overlays and will provide resources in a 'dyslexic-friendly' font.

Potential exam access arrangements may include 25% extra time, a reader/computer reader (to read the exam questions aloud), someone to scribe for your child and/or a laptop.

Further support

Talk to your child's teacher or SENDCO

British Dyslexia Association
www.bdadyslexia.org.uk

The Dyslexia-SpLD Trust
www.thedyslexia-spldtrust.org.uk

BECOMING AN AWARD-WINNING WRITER WITH DYSLEXIA

Andy describes his own struggles as an undiagnosed dyslexic child, as well as how he's flourished as a dyslexic adult.

When I started rock climbing, my deep sense of spatial awareness and capacity to see through practical problems quickly propelled me to a high level of ability. This led me to take on harder and harder climbs, eventually pushing world-class limits.

Unlike climbing however, writing did not come easily to me. I am severely dyslexic and left school with barely a handful of O levels. In my first book, *Psychovertical* (Kirkpatrick, 2008), I describe how difficult I found school. I discuss how I found the school system to be set up to favour the very things I found most difficult – words and numbers – and how I routinely felt unintelligent, out of place and misunderstood and underestimated by my teachers. I left school feeling I lacked precisely what was most valued by society and feared I was facing a life on the dole.

A chance comment at a party led me to a diagnosis of dyslexia aged 19. I began to understand why I found some things easy and others impossible. When I eventually tried to write as a climber, I knew it would be difficult but persisted nevertheless. I took a painstaking two years to articulate the story I wanted to tell for my first 2000-word article. After much (literal) blood, sweat and tears, my achievements in writing now match those of my climbing career.

I see mine as an *against-all-odds* success story. The education system is now much better at identifying and supporting pupils with dyslexia but is still weighted in the way I experienced it – it still needs to be better at valuing a more diverse range of aptitudes.

By definition, not everyone can be world-class in their chosen field, but I hope my story can be an inspiration to teachers, pupils and parents.

A PARENT'S VIEW – GETTING A GRIP
ON DYSLEXIA LATER IN LIFE

Philippa shares how her diagnosis as an adult transformed her view of herself and helps her to empathize with her neurodivergent son.

I quite clearly remember at primary school really loving certain topics – especially science. As I made my way through school and we were streamed according to ability, however, I noticed I was never 'on the top table', and I was given some additional support for handwriting and reading.

In secondary school, my struggles became more pronounced, and I didn't know what to do with the feedback I received for topics such as English. I was told I had poor grammar and spelling but I couldn't really understand what the problem was or how to improve it. I started to struggle with every subject – even science. As I moved towards my GCSEs, I felt incredibly stressed about not feeling able to get the results I needed to do A levels.

Despite working very hard and spending much of my time studying, I was put on foundation papers for several subjects, meaning the maximum grade I could get was a C. I had to really persuade my English teacher to let me try to complete a higher paper for English literature (for which I actually got an A).

Late recognition of my difficulties

For my A levels, I struggled again with the massive jump – spending all my time in the library. And then one day my English literature teacher said to me, 'I think you might be dyslexic – everything is there but it's like a jumper all knitted together in the wrong way.' Unfortunately, this was just before my exams and no additional support was available. I was officially diagnosed by an educational psychologist at university but all that meant was I got more time to complete exams.

The game changer for me happened when I learned more about dyslexia in my 30s, when doing my postgrad. Now I understand why it takes me so long to absorb written information, and I tend to use a lot of videos now to help me get a grip of new topics. I have since achieved distinction grades at postgraduate level, having achieved a 2:2 in my first degree.

If I had known what I know now when I was younger – and been helped by knowledgeable teachers – maybe studying wouldn't have been so difficult. I now know I wasn't stupid and my brain just works in a different way. Figuring out how to work with my dyslexic brain was the key to achieving my potential. And now, as a parent of a neuro-divergent child, I feel much better prepared to support him because of my own experiences. I think it's important we are responsive to children and I'm glad there is better recognition of differences now.

Dyspraxia (developmental coordination disorder – DCD)

Dyspraxia describes people who have motor (movement) performance that is substantially below expected levels for their age and relative to their previous opportunities for skill acquisition. It is the result of disruption in communication between the brain and the body. This may manifest as poor balance and clumsiness, and significant delays in achieving developmental milestones such as walking, crawling and sitting. Acquisition of basic motor skills such as catching, throwing and jumping is likely to take longer, as will developing fine motor skills such as writing and cutting with scissors. Attention span may also be affected, as may the ability to follow instructions and manage the time and steps needed to carry out a task. It may also affect the ability to accurately keep up with the back-and-forth of a conversation.

Verbal dyspraxia is a related condition to describe difficulties with the precise movement needed to produce clear speech. It may appear alongside DCD.

About 5% of children are affected by dyspraxia. The precise cause is not understood; however, it is more common in people who were born early, had a low birth weight and have a family history of coordination difficulties (Dyspraxia Foundation, 2023).

Diagnosis

Referral to an occupational therapist, physiotherapist or paediatrician can be made through your child's SENDCO or GP. Potential verbal dyspraxia can be assessed by a speech therapist. Diagnosis will typically consist of assessing movement and history-taking. Overlap with other conditions such as autism is common, and professionals take this into account when identifying the most appropriate diagnosis. It is not always possible to arrive at a formal diagnosis of dyspraxia. However, the assessment process is important anyway because it may enable parents and professionals to more fully understand your child and to identify the most appropriate support.

A PARENT'S VIEW – OUR SON AND SPEECH DYSPRAXIA

A parent describes how speech difficulties are part of who his son is.

Our son didn't communicate with words until he was three. Even when he did start communicating with words, his speech has been quite muffled and is tricky to understand – particularly out of context. He also tends to use the same consonant sounds for a range of letters. You really have to 'tune in' to his speech to be able to follow it.

An ongoing journey towards diagnosis

When he was younger, he wasn't diagnosed with anything in relation to his speech. However, when he was a little older and started school, the speech therapist diagnosed a 'speech sound disorder'; we guess because his speech didn't become clearer over time like is often the case with young children. Now he is six, and another speech therapist has suggested he may have verbal dyspraxia. The difference in practice doesn't seem all that clear, but we understand the cause to be related to planning and coordinating movements in the brain as opposed to muscle weakness or physiological differences in the body. His use of language is therefore different because he thinks differently. Coupled with the unclear diction, his speech can be really hard for people who don't know him well to understand.

He has been referred to the Nuffield Centre – a specialist speech clinic – for more assessments and to ascertain whether he would benefit from any particular kind of help.

The way he speaks makes life difficult for him and he often gets frustrated if we don't understand him; but despite this, we do love the way he talks and it is very much part of who he is. There is nothing quite like hearing his pronunciation of 'duck-billed platypus' for example, or the fact that for some reason he calls sausage rolls 'roll sausages'. We often adopt these idiosyncrasies within our family, much to the bemusement of outsiders!

Help that your child may receive at school

Dyspraxia can affect children's ability to fully participate in learning and school life, either directly or because of resulting anxiety or lack of confidence. It is therefore important that schools work to support pupils as best they can to prevent low self-esteem and a reluctance to engage in learning. Teachers might: make allowances in the arrangement of the classroom and in terms of where children sit, explain tasks step by step and use visual aids, allow extra time to complete tasks and provide technology such as iPads to support communication and literacy. If your child is supported by an occupational therapist, they will advise the class teacher and may also give specific exercises that can support fine or gross motor skill development.

Exam access arrangements may include a practical assistant (to support practical tasks), a laptop, a scribe/speech recognition software and/or 25% extra time.

Further support
Go to your health visitor or GP
Talk to your child's teacher or SENDCO
Dyspraxia Foundation (although the Dyspraxia Foundation closed in 2024, its website is still available as a source of advice and resource)   https://dyspraxiafoundation.org.uk

Hearing impairment

A person is said to have hearing loss if they are not able to hear as well as someone with normal hearing, meaning hearing thresholds of 20 dB or better in both ears. It can be mild, moderate, moderately severe, severe or profound, and can affect one or both ears (World Health Organization, 2021).

Diagnosis

Referral to an audiologist will typically be through the child's GP. In many parts of the country, hearing tests are also carried out routinely when children start school.

Help that your child may receive at school

Children with a hearing impairment may well receive support that is unique to their own profile of hearing loss and the resultant communication methods most effective for them. It may be that they have equipment to support hearing, such as a radio aid that works with their hearing aid. It may be that methods such as British Sign Language (BSL) become the child's primary source of communication.

While many children with a hearing impairment will have no impairment of cognitive function, the development of vocabulary can falter if not adequately supported. A school may pay extra attention to vocabulary acquisition in order that the child doesn't fall behind their peers in the curriculum. A teacher would typically check in with a pupil with a hearing aid more frequently than their peers so that they do not make assumptions about what has been communicated; they would typically use visuals as a core aspect of classroom learning.

The school will look to create a classroom environment in which your child's communication preferences are embedded in daily routines. Additional work may also go into ensuring that your child's hearing impairment does not cause them any social isolation.

Possible exam access arrangements may include a communication professional (e.g., to transcribe your child's BSL answer), a scribe, extra time and/or supervised rest breaks.

Further support

Go to your health visitor or GP

Talk to your child's teacher or SENDCO

National Deaf Children's Society
www.ndcs.org.uk

Moderate learning difficulties

Pupils with moderate learning difficulties (MLD) will have attainments well below expected levels in all or most areas of the curriculum, despite appropriate interventions. They will have much greater difficulty than their peers in acquiring basic literacy and numeracy skills and in understanding concepts (Department for Education and Skills, 2003).

The term first appeared in the UK education system in the 1978 Warnock Report. It is now the fourth most prevalent primary need type in English schools (National Statistics, 2024).

In reality, the term MLD is sometimes used by schools when no particular medical diagnosis has been given and when screeners do not show that the main block to a child's learning is specific (e.g., dyslexia) or language-based (e.g., developmental language disorder). It will typically be used by a school, often without medical evidence, when a child struggles in many aspects of their learning. Typically, a child with MLD may struggle to: learn, use and retain new vocabulary; process new information; possess the skills for substantial levels of independence when working; keep information in their working memory; and access the literacy demands of a curriculum.

Diagnosis

MLD may be diagnosed following a multidisciplinary assessment undertaken by clinicians in a Child Development Centre. This diagnosis is likely to be the result of some cognitive testing (depending on the child's age and current ability), some observation and an account from the parent and school. Many children will be given a label of MLD by the school without having received a formal diagnosis.

Help that your child may receive at school

For pupils with MLD, the school's response will typically be high-quality teaching and targeted intervention. In the classroom, the teacher may take extra steps to break down tricky concepts, to pre-teach vocabulary and to communicate instructions. They may allow additional processing time when asking questions and they might be selective about what they teach, ensuring the core knowledge is clear rather than trying to teach every aspect of a curriculum.

It is possible that a child with MLD will access some additional academic intervention in school that is targeted at their area of need. This might be revisiting basic literacy and numeracy, going back over things learned in class that week or teaching upcoming vocabulary.

Possible exam access arrangements may include extra time of 25%, a reader/computer reader and a scribe/speech recognition technology.

Further support

Go to your health visitor or GP

Talk to your child's teacher or SENDCO

National Association for Special Educational Needs
www.nasen.org.uk

Oppositional defiant disorder

While all children have moments of defiance, the clinical threshold for a diagnosis of oppositional defiant disorder (ODD) talks of a period of months, with several symptoms and across multiple contexts. The NHS website (2021b) talks of ODD being, 'defined by negative and disruptive behaviour, particularly towards authority figures, such as parents and teachers'.

This may describe the needs of a child who typically falls foul of a school's behaviour policy.

In order for the child to be successful, they will need a school in which staff have the skills to maintain high expectations of respectful behaviour while knowing that they must make frequent reasonable adjustments to accommodate the child's needs. A child with ODD is less likely to consistently make and maintain positive relationships with peers and adults, more likely to struggle to manage conflicts successfully and less likely to stay calm and regulated throughout their school day.

Diagnosis

The diagnostic process typically starts with the child's GP, who might refer to a child psychiatrist in order to get the diagnostic ball rolling. Asking the school and parent to give their view will typically form a part of the process of assessment.

Help that your child may receive at school

When your child has ODD, a school will think very carefully about how to keep them calm and regulated throughout their day. They will do this partly through removing the unknowns, for example, by embedding consistent routines in lessons and through your child working with known and trusted adults. They might seek to remove the 'me against them' mentality that can be fostered by a child with ODD, perhaps by offering an element of choice when a child is completing their work.

A child with ODD may feel a greater sense of shame than other pupils, leading to situations potentially escalating quickly. A school will look to avoid this by issuing sanctions discreetly, by emphasizing the positive wherever possible and by very carefully sanctioning a specific behaviour, rather than the child in general.

Exam access arrangements may include withdrawal to a smaller room, a prompter to support focus and attention and/or supervised rest breaks.

Further support

Go to your health visitor or GP

Talk to your child's teacher or SENDCO

LANCUK
www.lanc.org.uk

Very Well Mind
www.verywellmind.com

Pathological demand avoidance

There is still relatively little known or written about pathological demand avoidance (PDA). If a clinician has spoken to you about your child potentially having 'a profile of PDA', that might have been the first time that you heard the term (unlike, e.g., autism or dyslexia).

Whereas every child can be avoidant when they have demands placed upon them, PDA is 'characterised by an avoidance of the ordinary, everyday demands of life' (Truman, 2021, p.15). Though there is no universal agreement about the nature and characteristics of PDA, it is typically diagnosed (or at least recognized) in some people who are also autistic, i.e., 'autistic with a PDA profile' or 'autistic with a demand avoidant profile' (National Autistic Society, n.d.).

The level of demand avoidance can be chronic in those who have a profile of PDA. The child typically feels anxiety about others' expectations in what many of us would perceive as normal demands, for example, wearing clothing appropriate for a certain setting, greeting a relative, sitting at the table. The pathological nature of PDA can lead to behaviours that it's hard for the non-PDA brain to rationalize, for example, a child not engaging in a favoured activity, because they feel that others expect them to enjoy it; a child not accepting praise, because they feel that the praise comes from meeting someone else's demands (that they enter a classroom quietly, that they complete all their work, that they behave calmly at the shops, etc.).

Diagnosis

PDA is typically diagnosed by a psychologist, though there is not one standardized assessment pathway for PDA. Its existence outside of standard diagnostic manuals means there is a lot of variation around almost every aspect of PDA, for example, whether or not someone will diagnose it in the first place, what tools they use to diagnose it and what terms they use when diagnosing it.

A starting point for a family member might be to raise the matter with the clinician with whom they're already working, be it a psychologist or paediatrician. The most informed person you could speak to about PDA is likely the same person you're talking to about your child's autism.

Help that your child may receive at school

Any adult working with a child with PDA will be considering the expectations and demands they place upon them. A teacher will consider where small but consistent tweaks to their communication might reduce the demands felt by the child. Rather than stating the (e.g.) three things a pupil must do and how they must do them (an external demand that the child is likely to avoid), teachers might offer choice, inviting the pupil to find their own strategy or to choose the order in which to complete tasks.

It may be that far more substantial changes are needed in school, perhaps through a teacher offering a much more personalized timetable. Additional adult support, and/or the use of a space outside of the mainstream classroom, may be used for pupils who struggle significantly when it comes to meeting demands.

Exam access arrangements might include a withdrawal room, a prompter and supervised rest breaks.

Further support

Talk to your child's teacher or SENDCO

Speak to the clinician involved in assessing your child for autism

National Autistic Society
www.autism.org.uk

PDA Society
www.pdasociety.org.uk

Physical disability
Diagnosis
Need will be diagnosed through specialist clinical assessment. The Equality Act (2010) defines a physical disability as: 'A limitation on a person's functioning, mobility, dexterity or stamina that has a "substantial" and "long-term" negative effect on an individual's ability to do normal daily activities.'

Help that your child may receive at school
It will be vital that the school your child is in has a good understanding of your child's physical needs and abilities. They are then legally obliged – as with any disability – to remove any substantial disadvantage.

In reality, that means your child being able to access other parts of the school building along with their peers, being able to participate in the same extracurricular opportunities as their peers and being given opportunities to access the same curriculum as their peers.

It is likely that a combination of an accessible school environment (e.g., ramps instead of stairs), adult support (e.g., to support with longer written tasks), consideration of the classroom environment (e.g., working at a desk with ease of access into the classroom) and specialist equipment (e.g., a writing slope, technology to support communication) will increase access for a child with a physical disability. Ongoing communication between the family, school and child, informed by your child's unique strengths and difficulties, is most likely to support successful educational provision.

Exam access arrangements may include a practical assistant (to support practical tasks), a laptop, a scribe/speech recognition software and/or 25% extra time.

Further support

Talk to your child's teacher or SENDCO

pdnet
www.pdnet.org.uk

Speech, language and communication needs

This broad group of needs is the most prevalent in English schools' SEND registers and is also the most common in primary schools. It describes a group of pupils who may have difficulties in:

- producing speech sounds
- using language to communicate (expressive language)
- understanding what is being said (receptive language)
- understanding or using the social rules of communication.

As you'll see from this list, the potential breadth of difficulties experienced by the child might have a significant impact on their ability to be understood, to understand others and to successfully access a curriculum.

Diagnosis

Many schools will work closely with a SALT in order to diagnose a condition such as a speech sound disorder or developmental language disorder. It is certainly common practice for schools to either commission their own SALT assessments or to refer to a local authority service. If a child has not yet started school, the local SALT service may well be accessed via the GP.

Help that your child may receive at school

Your child's class teacher will pride themselves on the clarity of their communication, being succinct with their language and pre-teaching the key words that may be unfamiliar to the pupil. They may rely additionally on visual supports (pictures, diagrams, etc.) to lessen the burden on receptive language skills and to use the child's 'visual channel' as a way for them to remember content.

For pupils with speech sound difficulties, schools will often take specialist advice from a SALT. A teacher will also create an environment of acceptance within their classroom while also repeating back a correct model of speech to the child. They will build a relationship with the child so that they still attempt full sentence answers in spite of a difficulty with speech. Additional intervention to support the production of speech sounds may well be possible, usually after the child has had access to some specialist assessment, accessed initially through a GP or school referral.

When it comes to understanding language, additional support may also be given to access reading comprehension tasks.

Possible exam access arrangements include extra time of 25%, a reader/computer reader and/or a scribe/speech recognition technology.

Further support
Go to your health visitor or GP
Talk to your child's teacher or SENDCO

Speech and Language UK
https://speechandlanguage.org.uk

Tourette's syndrome

Those of us of the reality TV generation remember Tourette's syndrome bursting into public consciousness in *Big Brother* 7 in 2006. The winner, Pete Bennett (1982–), has Tourette's syndrome. It was the first time most of the general public had thought about the condition. Pete's Tourette's was partially characterized by coprolalia – the utterance of obscene words or socially inappropriate and derogatory remarks – which is actually quite rare.

Most people with Tourette's have predominantly motor tics such as blinking and coughing. The condition tends to develop in childhood or adolescence and affects up to 1% of people. Because it can be mild, many cases go undiagnosed; its effects tend to decrease in severity towards adulthood.

What causes Tourette's is not known for sure, but it is thought to involve genetic and environmental factors. It occurs because of a change in certain neural circuits.

Treatments can vary depending on how the condition is affecting someone. In many cases, once the condition is understood, no further treatment is necessary. In more serious cases, behavioural therapy or drugs may be offered.

People with Tourette's may also have obsessive compulsive disorder (OCD), ADHD or learning difficulties. It is important that any co-occurring conditions are understood in order to best support the individual. As with many forms of SEND, more boys than girls are diagnosed with the condition.

Diagnosis

Diagnosis is made by a specialist doctor. You may decide to contact your GP if your child develops tics. Sometimes, children develop tics that do not persist, and Tourette's is not diagnosed.

Help that your child may receive at school

Teachers should be broadly supportive and not require your child to suppress their tics. Children may need additional help to stay focused and be assigned shorter tasks. If necessary, they should be allowed more breaks for movement. When a child is struggling greatly with their tics, it can be useful if they have the choice to temporarily leave their classroom to both reduce any external pressure they are feeling and to tic freely without feeling any self-consciousness about doing so in front of their peers.

Learning should be adapted if your child finds it hard to keep information and instructions in mind and to plan their work.

As tics are often more intense for the child when they are feeling stressed or anxious, schools should work hard to understand the root causes of a child's anxiety in school and any potential soothers (calming activities, adults to check in with, sensory tools to use) during times of anxiety.

Social situations can be difficult for people with tics. In some cases, it can lead to bullying. Schools should support social inclusion and have clear and effective ways to counter and deal with bullying if it does occur.

Possible exam access arrangements may include withdrawal to a smaller room and supervised rest breaks, which both aim to reduce the potential anxiety faced by the child during an exam and/or reduce the impact of the child's tics on other pupils.

Further support
Contact your GP
Your child's teacher or SENDCO

Tourette's Action
www.tourettes-action.org.uk

Visual impairment

It's common for children to need glasses or contact lenses: about a quarter of children use them. This alone does not mean they would be classed as having a special need related to their vision. The job of the glasses is to take care of the need and enable them to see clearly.

Visual impairment, on the other hand, is more serious and cannot be corrected with standard glasses or contact lenses. Visual impairment or low vision is a severe reduction in vision that reduces a person's ability to function at certain or all tasks. If a child is born with visual impairment, it is likely to be identified when they are quite young.

At school, a visual impairment can affect children across the board – not just in their ability to read and access visual learning materials. It can have a massive effect on a child's social world and their confidence, and it could get in the way of inclusion in sport, for example. Schools should do everything they can to mitigate these effects and to ensure your child can access all elements of school alongside their peers, albeit with some adaptations.

Diagnosis

A referral to specialist optometry or ophthalmology services can be accessed through the child's GP or via initial assessment from an optician.

Help that your child may receive at school

Like with all special needs, the support provided will need to match the particular needs of the child. However, it is likely that teachers will need to adapt the materials they use and the format in which they are provided. There might be specialist software that is useful, and your child may be able to produce their own work in different ways. The classroom (and wider school) environment may well be adapted to support your child to be safe and to maintain appropriate levels of independence.

The school might well work with you on how best to support your child's learning at home and inform you of how they go about things in the classroom.

Visually impaired children usually need different exam conditions. Possible exam access arrangements include exam papers printed in Braille/with enlarged texts, a reader/computer reader, a scribe/speech recognition technology and 25–50% extra time.

Further support
Speak to your GP or health visitor
Royal National Institute of Blind People www.rnib.org.uk
Royal Society for Blind Children www.rsbc.org.uk

CHAPTER 2

SCHOOLS AND THE EDUCATION SYSTEM

The previous chapter detailed some of the many types of support that schools give to pupils when they have a learning need of some kind. While we've looked at this for individual diagnoses, this chapter will give you a flavour of what schools do more broadly, across a wide range of school functions, when children have (or may have) SEND. If the majority of parents work with schools, nurseries or colleges for at least 12 years in relation to their child's learning, it's something you'll be very keen to know about.

Typically, children have spent at least 13,000 hours in school by the time they approach adulthood. Many of these children, with or without SEND, find school to be a platform for future happiness and lifelong success. In this chapter, we try to look at these 13,000+ hours from a SEND perspective. You will read about how you might choose a school for your child with SEND, what support you could typically expect from a school and how you might work with the school if your child is struggling in some way.

We also take you through some of the ways in which pupils might access additional support in school, including through an EHCP.

Finally, we look at some of the wider but still highly valuable parts of being a pupil in a school (completing work experience, going on residential trips), exploring some of the considerations and rights when it comes to pupils with SEND.

The national context
Talking numbers

A 'SEND register' is the term generally used by schools to describe their own log of the pupils they perceive to have SEND, some of whom will have a formal diagnosis. This information is shared with the Department for Education twice a year via the school census.

According to the most recent school census (National Statistics, 2024), there are over 1.5 million pupils on SEND registers in England.[1] This represents over 17% of all pupils or around five or six pupils per class. The most prevalent form of SEND is speech, language and communication needs, followed by social, emotional and mental health needs:

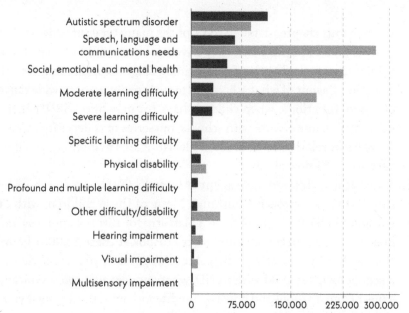

Number of pupils with an EHCP or SEN Support, by type of need, 2022/23

Note, the darker, top bar is for pupils with an EHCP; the lighter bar below it is for pupils who receive 'SEN Support' without an EHCP.

Source: National Statistics, 2023a, Number of pupils with an EHC plan or SEN Support, by type of need, 2022/23, used under Open Government license v3 www. nationalarchives.gov.uk/doc/open-government-licence/version/3 https://explore-education-statistics.service.gov.uk/find-statistics/special-educational-needs-in-england.

---

1   Plus: 242,000 pupils with 'additional support needs' in Scotland (Scottish Government, 2022); 63,000 with additional learning needs or SEN in Wales (Welsh Government, 2023); 64,500 in Northern Ireland (Northern Ireland Statistics and Research Agency, 2022).

EHCPs and SEN Support

Over 4% of pupils – or around one per class – have an EHCP, usually indicating that they have a more significant need and therefore require a higher level of additional or different provision in school. See page 74 for more information about EHCPs and how they can be applied for.

The rest of the pupils with SEND are on their school's SEND register but do not have an EHCP. They receive what the school will call 'SEN Support'. Some of these pupils will have a diagnostic label (e.g., someone will have diagnosed them as dyslexic), but others will not. Their school will probably not receive any additional money linked specifically to them as an individual, but the school still has a duty to use their 'best endeavours' to ensure needs can be met[2] and a legal duty to ensure anyone meeting the Equality Act (2010) (see page 72) definition of disabled is not placed at a substantial disadvantage.

School placement

Around half of pupils with an EHCP are educated in a state-funded mainstream school, and the rest are educated in some form of special school, whether state run or independent:

School type	2015	2016	2017	2018	2019	2020	2021	2022	2023
Maintained nursery	0.1	0.1	0.2	0.1	0.1	0.1	0.2	0.2	0.2
State-funded primary	26.2	25.5	25.8	26.3	27.4	28.3	29.4	29.7	30.3
State-funded secondary	24.6	23.5	22.2	20.9	20.4	20.4	21.0	21.6	22.4
State-funded special	41.4	42.9	43.8	44.2	43.8	42.6	40.6	39.4	37.9
State-funded AP schools	0.7	0.6	0.7	0.7	0.8	0.9	0.9	0.9	0.9
Independent	5.3	5.7	5.8	6.3	6.1	6.4	6.7	7.0	7.4
Non-maintained schools	1.6	1.6	1.5	1.4	1.3	1.3	1.2	1.1	1.0

Percentage of pupils with a statement or EHC plan
by type of provision, England, 2015–2023

Source: Department for Education, 2023a, Percentage of pupils with a statement or EHC plan by type of provision, England, 2015–2023 table, used under Open Government license v3 www.nationalarchives.gov.uk/doc/open-government-licence/version/3.

---

2   Special schools and wholly independent schools do not have this 'best endeavours' duty.

It's helpful to note a couple of elements behind this number:

- Local authorities (who have responsibility for delivering the provision specified in 'Section F' of an EHCP) may be less likely to want to fund 'independent' placements – think private special schools. Placements in such a school may cost more to the local authority than a place in a school that the local authority manages and/or at which they have already commissioned their places for the year.
- Within 'state-funded primary/secondary' are mainstream schools that host a 'Specialist Resource Provision'. See the section 'Choosing a school' on page 85 for more on this.

Pupils who have SEND but no EHCP (with needs being met at the 'SEN Support' level) are almost exclusively educated in mainstream schools; they are sometimes educated in 'alternative provision' but rarely in special schools. It is highly likely that if you want your child to go to a special school, they will first require an EHCP to be in place.

Are there more children with SEND now?

There are some people over a certain age who may tell you that autism didn't used to exist or that special needs weren't a thing 'when I went to school'. Are they right?

No, they're most certainly wrong. It's worth unpicking recent increases in identification, however.

Using autism as a particular example, we know that there has been a dramatic increase in diagnosis. One UK study found there to be a 787% increase in autism diagnoses between 1998 and 2018 (Russell et al., 2022).

We know that public awareness of terms such as ADHD, dyslexia and dyspraxia has increased greatly.

And we know that the number of pupils on the SEND registers of English schools has been slowly increasing for the past seven years or so (Department for Education, 2024b).

So, on paper, we know that the number of people with SEND in the UK, including the number of children, has increased. We do not have a conclusive answer as to whether that should be celebrated as an increase in societal acceptance of neurodivergence, social understanding of SEND and clinical access to SEND assessment or seen as a real sign of increased need, or perhaps a little of both.

Over-represented groups

In England, it's true that some groups are over-represented on the SEND registers of schools. Here are some examples:

- Boys are over-represented on SEND registers by a ratio of around 2:1.
- Children from lower-income households are around twice as likely to be on a SEND register.
- There is a great difference in the percentage of children on SEND registers according to ethnicity, with some ethnic groups greatly over-represented.
- Pupils with English as an Additional Language are slightly under-represented on SEND registers in England.
- Children who are Looked After (i.e., they are cared for by their local authority in some regard) are greatly over-represented on SEND registers.
- There is also evidence to suggest that a child is more likely to appear on a SEND register if they're 'summer born' (see below).

National Statistics (2023a)

SUMMER BORN OR SEND?

The Education Select Committee heard in 2015 that children born in August are 90% more likely to be placed on a SEND register (Camden, 2015).

It's easy to understand why an August-born child may struggle more in some aspects of their learning than a September-born peer, particularly in the earliest years of their schooling. When they start school, they've been alive for 20% less time!

Some summer-born pupils will be correctly identified as having SEND, but the statistic above tells us that there will also be cases of incorrect identification. As a parent, being aware of this fact may help you when thinking about the school's work to support your child, especially when it comes to conversations about whether or not their difficulties constitute SEND. A focus on current need and provision, rather than diagnostic label/placement on a SEND Register, is often more useful for many children in their youngest years.

The government's response

The Department for Education in England has responsibility for developing policy that supports pupils with SEND; SEND typically features on the portfolio of one minister from this department. In an attempt to improve the national state of provision, a review was announced in 2019 that looked at the state of affairs nationally and sought to recommend ways forward.

The state of the nation in relation to SEND

A governmental review of educational provision for children with SEND, published in 2022, found problems within the system, particularly highlighting three current challenges:

- **Challenge 1**: Outcomes for children and young people with SEND or in alternative provision are poor.
- **Challenge 2**: Navigating the SEND systems and alternative provision is not a positive experience for children, young people and their families.
- **Challenge 3**: Despite unprecedented investment, the system is not delivering value for money for children, young people and families.

HM Government (2022)

This 'SEND Review' found that the system wasn't working for pupils, for families or for taxpayers.

If you're reading this book, it's likely you are a family member of a child or young person with SEND. You may therefore have experienced Challenge 2 first-hand.

The scale of this challenge cannot be underestimated:

- Complaints from parents to the local ombudsman have been on the rise for many years (Department for Education, 2019; Tirraoro, 2023a).
- Parents are increasingly appealing local authority decisions (the decision not to provide an EHCP, the decision not to agree to fund a particular school) – and they're very often winning those appeals (Ministry of Justice, 2023).
- Waiting times to be assessed for various types of SEND are often unhelpfully long, and EHCPs are frequently not written within the legal timeframe (National Statistics, 2023b).

Too often, parents have to fight for things that should be their legal right.

Following this 'SEND Review' and the identification of these three challenges, the government published its 'SEND and Alternative Provision Improvement Plan' in 2023, articulating how it will aim to address the challenges mentioned above (Department for Education, 2023c).

Though the government has changed since the review, it's worth pausing for a moment to consider what these planned changes could look like for children and families in terms of placement, provision and paperwork:

National Standards: For many parents, there is an inconsistency in terms of SEND provision between their child's school and the 'school up the road', with the feeling that some schools 'do' SEND, while others don't have a duty to do this. A series of 'National Standards' should attempt to address this, outlining to schools and parents what every mainstream school should be able to do in relation to identifying SEND and meeting needs.

Upskilling the workforce: The Improvement Plan mentions the need for staff to receive additional, high-quality and evidence-informed training in relation to SEND so that many more needs can be met within mainstream classrooms.

A standardized, digitized EHCP process: Any veterans of the EHCP system may well have ring binders full of paperwork, filled with a multitude of forms from a range of agencies. The attempt will be to digitize this process and to standardize it nationally so that EHCPs (and the processes around them) don't feel different depending on where you live. It is hoped that standardizing the paperwork and processes will remove some of the current 'postcode lottery' in relation to parents' experiences of the SEND system.

More special schools: In addition to an expectation that mainstream schools are better placed to meet needs, there is also a commitment to increase the number of special schools.

Greater difficulty in getting an EHCP: There has been no legal change to the threshold at which a child should be entitled to an EHCP. However, the percentage of children who have one has increased from 2.6% to over 4% of children since 2016, an increase that is deemed unsustainable. There is a clear desire stated in this plan for this increase to slow down through needs being met earlier and at the 'SEN Support' level (i.e., the level before a child requires an EHCP).

For a more detailed summary of the plan, see this summary from the Special Needs Jungle website:

Special Needs Jungle – The Government's SEND Improvement Plan: An Initial Overview (Tirraoro, 2023b) www.specialneedsjungle.com/the-governments-send-improvement-plan-an-initial-overview

---

The full government document can be found here:

SEND and Alternative Provision Improvement Plan www.gov.uk/government/publications/ send-and-alternative-provision-improvement-plan

---

How schools support children with SEND

As a parent of a child with SEND, it can feel like there is a new language you need to learn. In addition to the glossary we've included on page 222, the following should provide an insight into how schools support pupils when they have SEND.

What to expect from your child's teacher(s)

The SEND Code of Practice (2015) is clear that teachers have a duty towards all pupils:

> Teachers are responsible and accountable for the progress and development of the pupils in their class.

> High quality teaching, differentiated for individual pupils, is the first step in responding to pupils who have or may have SEN.

Your child's teachers, therefore, should be able to talk to you about the progress your child is making. Even if your child has support from a teaching assistant, contact with the SENDCO or involvement from external agencies, responsibility for children's progress remains with their class teacher(s) first and foremost. Some of the teaching approaches they are likely to embed in their classroom are outlined in the section 'Common diagnoses', starting on page 26.

Whatever the teacher's level of experience or confidence with SEND, it is reasonable to expect them to know the answers to the following questions about your child:

WHAT SHOULD I ASK... WHEN SPEAKING TO THE CLASS TEACHER?

- Why is my child on the SEND register?
- What information about my child has been communicated to all adults who see them in school?
- What support is currently in place in order to meet their needs?

- How do you measure my child's progress, both academically and in terms of any targets related to SEND?
- When will I next be able to discuss my child's progress and provision with you?

There may well be questions that relate specifically to your child's level and type of SEND, for example:

- How are you supporting my child to communicate their needs?
- What additional literacy/numeracy support is my child receiving?
- How is my child being supported to develop peer relationships?
- How are you keeping my child safe while they are in school?

A positive relationship with the school may mean that you know the answers to these questions anyway or can find them out if not. They are not intended to be combative. A reflective, responsive school should not find these questions threatening, if they are asked appropriately, but should embrace the spirit of co-production and parent partnership that you are offering.

What to expect from a SENDCO

All mainstream schools are required to have a SENDCO (often spelled 'SENCO') – a SEN, or SEND, Coordinator. This is one of the few school roles that are mandated by the government, so any discussion you have with your child's school about SEND is likely to involve the SENDCO at some stage. Special schools do not have to have a SENDCO, and sometimes they don't – the mantra being that every teacher in a specialist setting takes the function of a SENDCO (to some degree) for the pupils in their class.

Although they must be qualified teachers, SENDCOs vary significantly. While one SENDCO may be a senior leader in the school (e.g., an assistant principal), another may not. While for one SENDCO, this might be their only role in school, for another SENDCO, it might sit alongside full-time classroom teaching duties. While one SENDCO might have a wealth of experience and passion with SEND, another SENDCO might have taken on the role due to a staff resignation or the school's very real budgeting pressures.

All SENDCOs are currently required to complete a postgraduate qualification[3] (the 'SENDCO NPQ'), but they have up to three years to complete it – meaning your child's SENDCO may have no specific or formal SEND qualification.

DUTIES OF A SENDCO

The key duties of a SENDCO include:

- overseeing the day-to-day operation of the school's SEN policy
- co-ordinating provision for children with SEN
- liaising with parents of pupils with SEN
- being a key point of contact with external agencies, especially the local authority and its support services
- liaising with potential next providers of education to ensure a pupil and their parents are informed about options and a smooth transition is planned
- working with the headteacher and school governors to ensure that the school meets its responsibilities under the Equality Act (2010) with regard to reasonable adjustments and access arrangements
- ensuring that the school keeps the records of all pupils with SEN up to date.

SEND Code of Practice (2015)

It's clear from this list that a SENDCO is not expected to be involved in every bit of support your child receives but has a vital leadership role in relation to coordination and oversight of provision.

---

3   This is true for all SENDCOs appointed after 1 September 2009 (Department for Education, 2024a).

WORKING ALONGSIDE PARENTS – THE PERSPECTIVE OF A PRIMARY SENDCO

Alana writes about the vital importance of building trusted relationships with families.

In our setting, we work with children aged 3–11 years, so we see a very broad spectrum of need. As SENDCOs, we need to be mindful that parents are on their own journey of understanding their child's needs and that this process, often filled with professionals and appointments, can be overwhelming.

Most of my work is with families who have very young children, and we are often joint partners in navigating the right support together. When working with families, I endeavour to form a shared understanding of a child's needs and of the approaches, strategies and resources that can support the child.

Using the expertise of parents

Consistency between home and school is crucial. When we work in harmony, we see the best outcomes for children.

I hope to build trusting relationships and have open, honest communication that is shared frequently. Any bit of information shared by parents is helpful, from whether the child had their normal breakfast to whether they had to take a different route to school due to traffic; from what language or visuals are working at home to whether there has been a change to the family dynamic. This insight is invaluable in helping us to understand a child and in ensuring we put in the best provision to meet their needs.

Alana Lloyd, Primary Deputy Headteacher and SENDCO

Depending on the way a school delivers this provision (and how large the school's SEND register is), the SENDCO may not be the person you speak to most about your child's SEND. This isn't necessarily an issue – you as a parent just need confidence that your child's SEND is being understood, considered and supported appropriately. If your child's SENDCO is working in a particularly pressured context (no time to do the role, many other hats to wear in school), this will first mean asking the school where the support is coming from and who your main point of contact should be in relation to SEND. This might be the class teacher, a teaching assistant who knows your child well and/or another member of staff.

Though the way the provision is delivered will vary from school to school, you might choose to discuss any or all of the following if you are sitting down with your child's SENDCO:

WHAT SHOULD I ASK... WHEN MEETING THE SENDCO?

- What information has been provided to the adults working with my child?
- What targets/outcomes is my child currently working towards?
- What provision is in place to meet my child's needs, and when can we review it?
- What can I do at home to increase the impact of your work in school?
- Do you plan to involve any external agencies in relation to my child's SEND?
- Does my child need an EHCP, or can their needs be met at the 'SEN Support' level?

What to expect from a teaching assistant

As a parent, it is hard to get used to not knowing what your child is doing every day. This is particularly the case when a child starts nursery, starts statutory education in Reception or starts secondary school. It can be even more the case when a child has SEND.

Knowing that a teaching assistant (TA) is working closely with their child can be a great comfort to parents. A teaching assistant gives parents reassurance that their child is not struggling alone; a TA might provide daily communication about the child's day (particularly important if the child is pre-verbal); a TA can deliver the interventions that a child needs.

ACCESSING TA SUPPORT FOR YOUR CHILD

There are many teaching assistants in English schools; they represent around 29% of the school workforce (National Statistics, 2023c). They are some of the most supportive, compassionate and resilient colleagues in the education system.

However, many parents need to have their expectations managed in terms of the TA support available to their child.

- Without an EHCP, close (i.e., one-to-one) TA support is unlikely to be affordable for a school.
- Even with an EHCP, the funding that comes with it may not be enough to provide a full-time additional adult in school.
- The vast majority of pupils with SEND are supported in school without one-to-one TA support, perhaps accessing support through a class TA or through interventions taking place outside the classroom, as well as through their regular classroom teacher(s).

IMPACTFUL TA PRACTICES

Though the presence of a teaching assistant can provide great reassurance, parents should be cautious about overstating the importance of a teaching assistant for all children. Although teaching assistant support is vital for some children, and although the practices of TAs can be transformative for pupils, it can also be the case that:

- at worst, TAs create a learned helplessness in children with SEND. There are studies that show that if two children have the same type and level of SEND, the child without TA support can fare better than the child with TA support (Blatchford *et al.*, 2009)
- at worst, teachers abdicate responsibility for educating a child with SEND to a TA rather than taking full responsibility for the child's learning as they would for other pupils
- at worst, the presence of a TA denies the child opportunities to interact with peers and brings additional stigma to their need for additional support.

Now, of course, a great deal of TA practices are not 'at worst', and:

- at best, TAs are well trained, work in close partnership with the teacher and provide the 'least help first', maintaining an expectation that the child will work as hard as they can, listen as attentively as they are able to and only have additional help when it is required
- at best, TAs support a pupil's ability to develop greater independence over time, to succeed in peer interactions and to recognize and request help when they need it.

If your child does have a teaching assistant working with them, you might want to ask them the following questions:

WHAT SHOULD I ASK... A TEACHING ASSISTANT?

- What have you noticed my child does well at school?
- How can I help you to better understand my child?
- What training or support have you received (or are you due to receive) that will help you to work with my child?
- What targets/outcomes are you supporting my child with?
- What is the best way for us to maintain open channels of communication?
- How are you trying to build up my child's ability to do things for themselves where appropriate?
- How are you supporting their social inclusion within the class?

Ultimately, teachers have a responsibility for all learners, irrespective of whether there is an additional adult in the classroom. Having a TA work with your child can be incredibly helpful, but the teacher's duty to lead your child's learning remains in place regardless.

Support in exams

Schools have a duty to track the progress of children. In certain school years, this involves formal testing, with results being reported to the Department for Education.

- **Reception**: The Early Learning Goals
- **Year 1**: Phonics screening check
- **Year 2**: Key Stage 1 SATs (these are no longer statutory, so some schools will no longer ask their pupils to sit these)
- **Year 4**: Multiplication tables check
- **Year 6**: Key Stage 2 SATs
- **Year 11**: GCSE (and equivalent) exams
- **Year 13**: A level (and equivalent) exams

It should perhaps be stressed that in younger years, this does not look like formal examination in the way we might remember from our own schooling. It is assessed in an ongoing manner in Reception, as one-to-one spoken assessment in Year 1, etc.

With all types of formal assessment in schools, there is capacity for schools to adjust the assessment in order to remove a disadvantage. It is not about giving pupils the answer, but it's about supporting the child to be able to take the examination in a way that better allows them to demonstrate their potential.

Some of the most common types of 'exam access arrangement' include:

- additional time (typically 25%)
- a different (typically smaller) room in which to complete the exam
- a reader/computer reader (so the child hears the questions spoken aloud)
- a scribe/speech recognition software
- supervised rest breaks (so the child takes the exam in chunks rather than all at once)
- a prompter (someone to give the pupil reminders to focus on the exam).

There is no exhaustive list of available arrangements, and it is not within the scope of this book to outline the specific guidelines/exemptions at each key stage, but the above list should make it easier for you to have a productive discussion with school about upcoming examinations, should you need to.

The rules around these exam access arrangements get a bit tighter as pupils get older.

In most cases, the child will only be allowed the arrangement in exams if it is their 'normal way of working'/'normal classroom practice', i.e., if they also have this arrangement, at least some of the time, during their day-to-day classroom learning.

In some cases, from GCSE onwards, the child will need to undergo a test, receiving a 'standardized score' in relation to a particular area of difficulty that will ascertain whether they are allowed to have the access arrangement (extra time, etc.) in examinations.

WHAT SHOULD I ASK... IN THE RUN-UP TO EXAMS?

- Will my child be taking the same exams as other children?
- How is my child being prepared for the exams so they can perform at their best in the exam?
- Will you be implementing any 'exam access arrangements' to support my child to perform to their full potential?

The legal framework for support

No parent should feel that they need to become a legal expert in order to support their child. Where it does feel like you need to be a legal expert, the excellent IPSEA website is a one-stop shop for explaining the law around SEND to parents and carers.

IPSEA

www.ipsea.org.uk

In terms of understanding relevant law, it is broadly useful for parents to be aware of the following:

The Equality Act (2010)

The Equality Act (2010) is the legal framework that supports the rights of disabled people. As one of the 'protected characteristics', disabled people must not be discriminated against. This right extends to all people and is therefore relevant to your child in a school, nursery or other setting.

Importantly, your child does not need to have any formal recognition of their disability (i.e., via a statutory document such as an EHCP or a funding arrangement such as Disability Living Allowance) in order to receive this protection. They must have a 'physical or mental impairment' that has a 'substantial and long-term adverse effect' on their ability to carry out 'normal day-to-day activities'.

In relation to disability, the Equality Act (2010) talks of 'reasonable adjustments' (schools and other institutions must, 'take such steps as it is reasonable to have to take to avoid the disadvantage'). These reasonable adjustments must be made in relation to a range of practices; such adjustment is as relevant to educational providers as it would be in adulthood for an employer.

As a parent, it can be useful to talk to your child's school about where reasonable adjustment is being made for your child.

The Children and Families Act (2014)

This legislation is the legal framework relevant to most schools and educational settings where children have SEN. Specifically, the school must 'use its best endeavours to secure that the special educational provision called for by the pupil's or student's special educational needs is made'.

The SEND Code of Practice (2015)

This piece of statutory guidance gives some detail to schools in relation to their SEND policies and practices. Where things are working well, it is likely that many of the things in place will align with the SEND Code of Practice's requirements on schools. In any situation of conflict, it is likely that one party (school, local authority, parent) will be leaning on the SEND Code of Practice to remind the school/local authority of what they may not be doing sufficiently well.

The legal duties to parents

Parents have rights protected in law when it comes to SEND, as written into the Children and Families Act (2014). The SEND Code of Practice (2015) articulates these when it tells schools what they 'must do' and what they 'should do' in relation to SEND. These duties are summarized below, with the 'must do' statements (i.e., the things that schools have a legal duty to deliver) in bold. The numbers refer to the corresponding sections within the SEND Code of Practice (2015):

- **Inform parents when making special educational provision for a child** (6.2) and agree the types of support, the expected impact and the expected review date (6.48).
- Help parents to understand what they can do at home to support any school-based interventions (6.51).
- Involve parents in decision-making (6.19).
- Listen to parents' concerns about their child's development (6.20, 6.45). Involve parents in a discussion around strengths, needs and outcomes and share a brief record of discussions (6.39).
- **Formally inform parents if a child is going on a SEN register (6.43)**.
- **Seek parental permission before contacting external professionals (6.47)**.
- Feed back to parents about the progress being made and consult parents about any changes to provision (6.54).
- Schools should meet parents at least three times per year (6.65).

In relation to this final point, it doesn't need to be the SENDCO who meets with you three times per year; the school may believe that someone else is more appropriate (a class teacher, a head of year). The guidance actually suggests that it is more likely to be the class teacher: 'These discussions should be led by a teacher with good knowledge and understanding of the pupil who is aware of their needs and attainment. This will usually be the class teacher or form tutor, supported by the SENCO.'

Education, Health and Care Plans

An EHCP is a statutory document for children and young people between the ages of 0 and 25. Around 5% of school-age children have an EHCP.

Amongst other things, an EHCP will outline:

- a child or young person's needs
- their desired outcomes (and the outcomes that others desire for them)
- the provision that must be in place in order to meet those outcomes.

It is designed to give statutory entitlement to a child or young person with a high level of SEND. It should guarantee them certain types of provision from education, health and/or social care providers and will typically provide some funding and/or access to local services.

The voices of the parent and the child take centre stage in an EHCP. In its creation, and at each 'annual review', it is vital that the views of both are documented and taken into account.

'Outcomes' is the term used to describe the longer-term targets for the child. These should articulate the direction of travel for the work that takes place with (and for) the child or young person. They should articulate what the child should be able to do within a given period of time.

If you think your child may need an EHCP

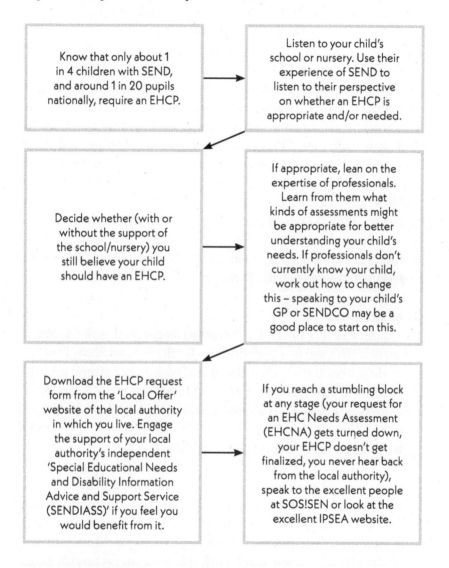

Know that only about 1 in 4 children with SEND, and around 1 in 20 pupils nationally, require an EHCP.

Listen to your child's school or nursery. Use their experience of SEND to listen to their perspective on whether an EHCP is appropriate and/or needed.

Decide whether (with or without the support of the school/nursery) you still believe your child should have an EHCP.

If appropriate, lean on the expertise of professionals. Learn from them what kinds of assessments might be appropriate for better understanding your child's needs. If professionals don't currently know your child, work out how to change this – speaking to your child's GP or SENDCO may be a good place to start on this.

Download the EHCP request form from the 'Local Offer' website of the local authority in which you live. Engage the support of your local authority's independent 'Special Educational Needs and Disability Information Advice and Support Service (SENDIASS)' if you feel you would benefit from it.

If you reach a stumbling block at any stage (your request for an EHC Needs Assessment (EHCNA) gets turned down, your EHCP doesn't get finalized, you never hear back from the local authority), speak to the excellent people at SOS!SEN or look at the excellent IPSEA website.

Requesting an EHCP

It's important to note that not all pupils with SEND require an EHCP in order to have their needs met. Around 19% of the school population are on SEND registers, with only about 1 in 4 of these children having an EHCP (the rest will be on the school's register as receiving 'SEN Support'). It's certainly worth getting the view of your child's school or nursery before considering whether an EHCP should be the goal.

In practice, schools most commonly make the request for an EHCNA on behalf of a child or young person and with the agreement and permission of their parents. However, others can apply also. Importantly, parents (or other family members) can apply on behalf of the child. This may be because parents have a strong desire to lead on such an application, because the school feels unable (or is currently unwilling) to make such a request or because a child is out of education.

Parents should also note that young people are entitled to make their own application if they are over compulsory school age and under 25 years old.[4] The SEND Code of Practice also notes that, 'anyone else can bring a child or young person who has SEN to the attention of the local authority, particularly where they think an EHCNA may be necessary' (SEND Code of Practice, 2015, 9.9). This might mean you as a parent working with a well-informed family friend, using a parent advocate or even engaging a willing relevant professional to make the request with you on behalf of your child.

How to apply

To request an EHCP (or, to use the correct language, to make 'a request for an EHCNA'), you must use the form for the local authority in which your child lives (rather than the one in which they attend school). The form will be found on the relevant local authority's 'Local Offer' website (see 'Finding out about local schools' later in this chapter, page 89). Though it's been proposed that one standard form is to be rolled out nationally, this is not yet in place.

The form should be self-explanatory. It will typically ask you a series of administrative questions (contact details, etc.) and will soon move on to the things you know and notice about your child – anything relevant from their history, their strengths, difficulties they experience, your own aspirations for them and/or their aspirations for themselves, etc.

If the EHCNA request is accepted, this does not necessarily mean an EHCP will follow, but it does mean that a comprehensive process of assessment should begin.

From the moment the application (or 'EHCNA request') is received by the local authority, a 20-week process begins. This process leads

---

4   Compulsory school age ends on the last Friday in June that falls in the academic year in which they turn 16. For example, for a child born on 23 September 2008, compulsory school age will have ended on 27 June 2025.

either to a finalized EHCP or to a decision that an EHCP is not required. See the diagram below and the subsequent pages to understand what should happen within this 20-week process.

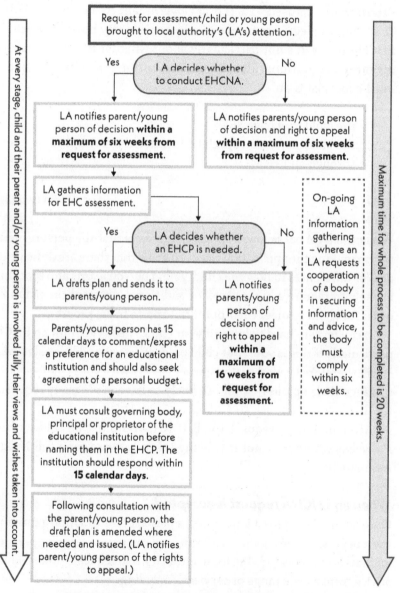

Source: SEND Code of Practice, Department for Education and Department of Health, 2015, 9.44. SEND Code of Practice 9.44 Request Assessment from local authority diagram used under Open Government license v3: www. nationalarchives.gov.uk/doc/open-government-licence/version/3.

Writing a successful application

Parents should be aware that many EHCNA requests do get accepted, but as with many things, there is regional variation here (Northumberland refused only 9.1% of EHCNA requests in 2022, whereas Peterborough refused 41% (Local Government Association, 2023)). That said, the legal bar for when a local authority must conduct an EHCNA is low. It's not particularly about whether the child has any diagnosed conditions. The person/institution making the request must show just that:

- the child may have SEN
- the child may need special educational provision to be made through an EHCP.

IPSEA (n.d.(a))

While the legal bar is low, in practice it means that the person/institution making the application needs to show that there are difficulties and/or differences in how the child/young person learns and that this is likely to require a higher level of additional/different provision in order for them to meet their potential and to make progress.

It can be very hard to know if your child's needs warrant an EHCP, particularly if this is your first child presenting with additional needs. It will therefore be vital that you work closely with your child's school to gauge their opinion – they are likely to have made many requests for EHCNA, and as such should have a useful view.

After making a request for EHCNA, you must be told within six weeks whether or not it is being taken forward for a full Needs Assessment.

When an EHCNA request is accepted

Once an EHCNA request is accepted, a period of information gathering then begins. The local authority informs the parents/young person, and views are collected. The local authority also requests professional advice from a wide range of services, including:

- the health service
- social care services within the local authority

- the headteacher/principal/manager of an early years setting, as appropriate.

If the local authority's decision is that an EHCP is being issued, it will first issue a draft. Though there is no weekly cut-off for this draft, they are normally issued by week 14 (starting from the moment the EHCNA request was received) in order for the parent and prospective/current school to each have 15 days to review this.

The final EHCP must then be issued within 20 weeks of the date that the application was received by the local authority.

When an EHCNA request is not accepted

Sometimes, an EHCNA request is turned down by the local authority. Sometimes, an EHCNA is agreed, but during that process, the local authority decides that an EHCP is not going to be issued (if this is the case, this decision must have been communicated by week 16). Both roads would lead to your child not receiving an EHCP.

If a request is turned down at either of these stages, parents have the right to appeal (Regulations 5 and 10 of 'The Special Educational Needs and Disability Regulations', 2014), even if they didn't make the initial request. Local authorities are duty-bound to inform parents of both the outcome and their right to appeal at both these stages.

If you would like to appeal, you might choose to engage the support of your local SENDIASS (see page 215). You might also choose to look at the very accessible 'Refusal to assess' pack from IPSEA, which gives advice to parents about the process of appeal.

IPSEA

www.ipsea.org.uk/refusal-to-assess-appeals

An appeal may result in mediation taking place between the local authority and the parent. Where stalemate continues, the decision not to assess/not to issue EHCP may go to a SEND First-Tier Tribunal (see page 83).

When an EHCP is agreed

Although EHCPs currently look different based on where in the country you are, the sections they must contain are the same:

Section A: The views, interests and aspirations of the child and his or her parents or the young person.

Section B: The child or young person's SEN.

Section C: The child or young person's health needs that are related to their SEN.

Section D: The child or young person's social care needs that are related to their SEN or to a disability.

Section E: The outcomes sought for the child or the young person. This should include outcomes for adult life. The EHCP should also identify the arrangements for the setting of shorter-term targets by the early years provider, school, college or other education or training provider.

Section F: The special educational provision required by the child or the young person.

Section G: Any health provision reasonably required by the learning difficulties or disabilities that result in the child or young person having SEN.

Section H1: Any social care provision that must be made for a child or young person under 18 resulting from Section 2 of the Chronically Sick and Disabled Persons Act (1970).

Section H2: Any other social care provision reasonably required by the learning difficulties or disabilities that result in the child or young person having SEN.

Section I: The name and type of the school, maintained nursery school, post-16 institution or other institution to be attended by the child or young person.

Section J: Where there is a personal budget, the details of how the personal budget will support particular outcomes, the provision it will be used for including any flexibility in its usage and the arrangements for any direct payments for education, health and social care. The SEN and outcomes that are to be met by any direct payment must be specified.

Section K: The advice and information gathered during the EHCNA must be attached (in appendices). There should be a list of this advice and information.

Your child's EHCP will contain the sections listed above.

TWO CONTRASTING EXPERIENCES OF GETTING AN EHCP

GETTING AN EHCP – A SIGNIFICANT CHALLENGE
Petra shares her own frustrating experience of getting an EHCP for her daughter.

At some stage in your journey, you may want additional assistance from your local council.

This could be additional support from a teaching assistant in the mainstream classroom or placement in a specialist school.

In the case of my three-year-old daughter, I completed the lengthy EHCP form to set about justifying why she needed help. In our case, we wanted her to be in a specialist school, as she had a lack of verbal communication (and other traits) and was not eating any solid food.

Completing the form
It is useful to have the support of your nursery/mainstream school/ professional diagnoses to support you in completing the form. A good grasp of the English language is helpful to explain why your

child needs help and how their day-to-day nuances require assistance (in our case) beyond the access of a mainstream school.

You should not be shy in stating all the problems your child has and giving cogent examples of the 'worst' behaviours. Be under no illusion: the council may try to refuse you/not give you funding for TA hours in the mainstream school or a place in a specialist school. The council has limited resources and depending on where you live, there are a lot of applicants for limited spaces. The application was not simple to complete nor easy to obtain.

Appealing the initial decision

For my daughter's application, once completed, we were informed that the council would provide the maximum hours to support her in a mainstream setting. Knowing my child, I knew she would not thrive or progress in a mainstream school. I decided to appeal the decision.

There was not a lot of information made available to us about appealing, so it was a voyage of discovery. In appealing, I was fortunate enough to come across our authority's SENDIASS, which independently advises parents in respect of appeals. The SENDIASS staff member told me to approach up to four specialist schools and let them see my daughter and speak to her nursery. I gave them access to the EHCP application so they could decide whether they would accept her.

The four schools saw my daughter, and three of them determined that they would accept her should the EHCP be amended to allow for a placement at a specialist school. In the background, I was taking steps to appeal the council's determination of her EHCP, but once the schools determined she would be a 'fit' for them, the council amended the EHCP. I avoided an appeal and she transitioned from nursery to the specialist school.

The application, on top of all the stresses you already have with your child with SEND, was by no means an easy, quick or stress-free process for us. We needed stubbornness, resolve and determination.

GETTING AN EHCP – WHEN THE SYSTEM WORKS

Stephen shares his own experience of getting an EHCP for his son – an experience in which community services worked effectively to identify, diagnose and get support in place.

For us and our son, the process of getting an EHCP was pretty straight-forward and was largely done on our behalf. He was diagnosed with this disability when he was three, having been referred to the local community paediatrics team. He attended a local authority nursery who had referred him when he was younger. All the agencies in our borough worked fairly well together, and we didn't have to push much for things to happen.

A nursery-led application

For the EHCP itself, the nursery school led on the application. Because they, the paediatrics team and the local authority were all linked, it wasn't really on the cards that the application wouldn't be taken forward. There was a kind of understanding that each was playing their part in identifying, assessing and supporting the children in the borough who needed it.

Our son was assessed by his nursery, speech therapists and an educational psychologist, as well as the paediatrician.

Choosing a school

When it came to naming the school, it was largely up to us. Although some of the professionals involved tried to point us in the direction of mainstream schools, we didn't have to 'fight' for a special school place. We visited all the local schools, including the special schools, and chose a special school that, luckily, was only a mile away. After reading his EHCP, the head teacher quickly evaluated that he would be accepted. There were other complications in the whole story, but we didn't really have to do anything to get the EHCP itself. We were involved along the way and our views were included in the final document. He had his EHCP by the time he was four and ready to start in Reception.

Exercising your rights through a tribunal

The SENDIST, or SEND First-Tier Tribunal, is an independent appeal panel that considers parental appeals against local authority decisions related to SEN (Children's Law Centre, 2020). These appeals might be around local authority's decision not to assess a child for an EHCP (an EHCNA), the decision not to issue an EHCP, changes within the plan or the decision to no longer maintain the plan.

A parent can challenge a decision around an EHCP at SENDIST. They may also bring a claim against a school to SENDIST if they believe that their disabled child is the victim of discrimination while at school. This can be the case irrespective of whether or not the child has an EHCP. In the latter instance, the case is about the school's approach/provision rather than being primarily about changing the content of an EHCP.

Personal budgets

In most cases, if your child receives educational support through an EHCP, any funding will go straight from the local authority to your child's nursery or school. However, personal budgets allow parents to have direct involvement in the financial operations here.

The SEND Code of Practice (2015, 9.95) says that a personal budget is, 'an amount of money identified by the local authority to deliver provision set out in an EHCP where the parent or young person is involved in securing that provision'.

A personal budget is a way in which parents/carers and young people can have more direct control over how the funding to meet the young person's needs is spent, where they have an EHCP. That said, only 3.7% of all EHCPs have a personal budget included within them (UK Parliament, 2023).

As a parent, you have a statutory right to be informed about the possibility of a personal budget.

That said, a personal budget is not an additional resource – it's just a resource that's provided differently. Think about how local authorities decide how much funding they will attribute to a given child for their provision – they decide it based on the needs of the child or young person. Therefore, a parent's request for a personal budget will not change the amount of provision (i.e., funding) on offer, as it does not affect the level of need of the child.

Any personal budget you request is therefore likely to take away resources from elsewhere. Furthermore, it can only be given in relation to special educational provision that is specified in Section F of an EHCP.

The examples below assume that the need for such provision is listed in Section F of your child's EHCP.

- A personal budget might be used to fund a private SALT of

your choice rather than using the preferred local authority/
in-school provider.

- A personal budget might be used to employ a tutor to provide
some additional support at home, with less of this support
being delivered by the school.

For some parents, accessing a personal budget increases the level of
choice available to them in regard to ensuring appropriate provision
for their child.

The vast majority of parents leave such choices to the education,
health and/or social care professionals involved in the delivery of the
EHCP.

Choosing a school

It is internationally acknowledged that a mainstream education should
be what countries aspire to provide for children with SEND:

> Those with special educational needs must have access to regular
> schools which should accommodate them within a child-centred
> pedagogy capable of meeting these needs.
>
> Regular schools with this inclusive orientation are the most effec-
> tive means of combating discriminatory attitudes, creating wel-
> coming communities, building an inclusive society and achieving
> education for all; moreover, they provide an effective education to
> the majority of children and improve the efficiency and ultimately
> the cost-effectiveness of the entire education system.
>
> United Nations (1994)

The UK Government is among the 92 governments that signed the
Salamanca Statement (quoted above) and is therefore committed to
children with SEND having access to 'regular schools' (i.e., mainstream
schools) for children with SEND.

In the UK, the Warnock Report (1978) made clear many years

earlier that pupils with SEND should ordinarily have their education provided within their local school, stating, 'we wholeheartedly support the principle of the development of common provision for all children' rather than them automatically having to go into a specialist setting whenever they have SEND.

The expectation that a mainstream education will be made available to all children has largely been held since the publication of that landmark report.

There can be tensions here though, of course. It is a noble aspiration that all children will be educated together, but the realities of this in practice (funding challenges, logistics, staff training, etc.) may in some cases mean that a child with special needs will do better in a special school than in a mainstream school. Some parents prefer the specialist approach, and some prefer the integrated approach. Each comes with advantages and disadvantages, and it is only possible to generalize to a limited degree. Ultimately, it is a personal decision based on your child and – more often than not – what is available in your area.

Parental choice

Choosing a school for your child is a very individual process. For a parent in a village with one primary school or a town with one secondary school, the idea of choice may feel false – in reality, there may be only one choice. For another parent, there may be a handful of schools that the child could realistically go to.

You may be choosing not only which school your child might go to but also what *type* of school they might go to – specialist, mainstream or mainstream with a Specialist Resource Provision, or indeed, whether they are home-schooled. For families, it can be really hard to gauge what the best option for a child might be.

The following might be useful in supporting you to understand the types of settings that may be available for your child:

Mainstream

These are schools that generally meet the needs of pupils across the ability range and with/without SEND. Although there may not be specialist staff on site permanently, schools still have a legal duty to make 'best endeavours' to deliver the provision their pupils require and to deliver education in a way that does not discriminate against pupils with SEND.

Specialist

Such schools generally have much smaller adult–child ratios, with teachers who have a greater level of SEND experience and with specialist staff (SALTs, etc.) on site for much or all of the week. They often have a specialism within one or two areas of SEND (autism, developmental language disorder, profound and multiple learning disorders, etc.). By definition, they provide less exposure to pupils who do not have SEND, but they will often closely target the life skills required for independence, and in practice, they will often find it easier to adapt their curriculum to the needs of an individual child than a mainstream school.

Mainstream with Specialist Resource Provision

If parents see their child attending a mainstream school but still accessing specialist support, a mainstream with a Specialist Resource Provision can be a good option. Look out for a range of names for such an arrangement; depending on the local authority, they may be called a Specialist Resource Provision (SRP), a Resource Base (RB) or an Additionally Resourced Provision (ARP).

Home-schooling

While it is clearly not a decision any parent takes lightly, it is the legal right of parents to educate their child at home if they should wish to. Officially known as 'Elective Home Education', there is no difference to the parent's legal rights when a child has SEND. If a parent of a child who receives SEN Support (i.e., no EHCP) would like to home-educate their child, they have a right to.

When a child has an EHCP, the legal right remains – but there is a bit more to know about around the duty of the local authority. Where the child has an EHCP, the local authority keeps its duty to maintain it (in reality, this duty extends to organizing an annual review process but often little else) but forgoes its duty to deliver the educational provision within it.

In short, that means that the local authority will not be funding a TA or sending a learning support teacher to your house – the duty to deliver the provision, and the duty to fund this provision, will often fall to you (see 'Education Otherwise Than at School', below, for exceptions to this rule).

Flexi-schooling

In effect, a more apt name would be 'part-time schooling'. Though all children have an entitlement to a full-time education, an arrangement can be reached whereby some of that education is organized (and delivered, usually) by the family, typically at home.

For a child with no EHCP, the school is under no obligation to agree to this. Parents are only legally allowed this arrangement with the school's consent.

For a child with an EHCP, the process needs to be agreed with the local authority, who would agree to such a move if it was inappropriate for some of the special educational provision to be provided in school (see 'Education Otherwise Than at School', below).

Education Otherwise Than at School

We wrote above that children with an EHCP can be home-schooled but the local authority's duty to deliver the provision no longer exists when parents choose to home-school. It's not quite 'you're on your own', but it's arguably not far off.

There is an exception. There may be a circumstance in which the child's needs *cannot be met in school*. This could be true for a child with high levels of anxiety about leaving their home, for example. In this case, the child may be eligible to receive Education Otherwise Than at School (EOTAS). If the parent can make a case (and if the local authority agrees) that physically attending a formal school building is inappropriate currently, the local authority has a duty to fund a provision that is likely to be largely at home.

For more information, see the EOTAS guide from SEND and You:

SEND and You – Education Other Than In School (EOTAS)
www.sendandyou.org.uk/wp-content/uploads/2022/02/
EOTAS-Resource-Final.pdf

Finding out about local schools

Local authorities are duty-bound to publish a Local Offer website. Among its many functions, a Local Offer website will detail the schools (including specialist schools) within the authority, information about school transport and a list of specialist services available to support children and families. An internet search naming your local authority and 'Local Offer' should bring you to the relevant website.

If you wish to learn more about schools within your area, your Local Offer website is a good place to start. It may be that local groups of parents are also a useful source of knowledge and first-hand experience about the provision available at a range of schools in the area.

Choosing a mainstream school

All schools hold events for prospective parents – open mornings or similar. It is always worth going to these events targeted at all parents (not only those whose children have SEND). You might look out for:

- whether the staff member telling you about the school (likely to be the head or a deputy) talks proudly of the school's work with pupils with SEND
- whether pupils with SEND appear to be present and included in the school.

You may also want to talk to someone about the school's SEND provision. Although any member of staff should be able to give you some level of answer about this, you may ask to book in a meeting with the SENDCO and to learn more about some of the specific things they do to support children with needs.

Whether at an open evening or a separate meeting with the SENDCO, you might choose to ask the following questions:

WHAT SHOULD I ASK... A MAINSTREAM SCHOOL AT THEIR OPEN EVENING?

- What kind of support do you provide for pupils, particularly when they are new to the school?

- What do teachers do in class in order to meet the needs of pupils?
- How are pupils with SEND included in all aspects of school life (assemblies, trips, etc.)?
- How do you work alongside families, particularly when children have SEND?

Particularly in a secondary school, you might also ask the following question:

- How does the SENDCO ensure that their knowledge about pupils gets shared with all teachers?

CHOOSING A SCHOOL FOR OUR SON
Stephen relays a story of primary school selection.

Our son fell into that broad category of 'could go to either', i.e., he had an EHCP and diagnosis and could attend a special school, but his needs were not so great that a mainstream school was out of the question. Making the decision was one of the most difficult things for us – much more so than the process of getting an EHCP or a diagnosis, both of which were straightforward in comparison.

I made the (perhaps naive) assumption that there would be some kind of system or process at the local authority to organize which children would be better suited to which kind of school. How wrong I was! We found out that basically it fell to us to make what seemed like the biggest decision of all: mainstream... or special?!

What made it all the more vexing was that although we could ask for 'professional advice' (from teachers, advisors, SENDCO, etc.), the advice was neither systematized nor consistent. Some – including his nursery teacher – pointed us in the direction of special, and others – namely his SENCO – said mainstream. We were told to visit schools and 'get a feel' for where we thought would suit our son. But this felt far too subjective and lacking in rigour.

I remember spending hours researching whether children had

better outcomes in mainstream or special, but I couldn't identify any relevant primary research. I was also surprised this wasn't a question more people were asking.

Coming to a decision

Having been round the houses with the whole thing and spent hours reading and listening to advice, I came to realize that the differences aren't particularly abstruse after all. There is no hocus-pocus going on in either sector. Both types of school are largely made up of adults doing their best to teach children the same kinds of things. Yes, there are differences, but there are also differences between mainstream schools.

Instead of asking esoteric questions, I wish I had sat down and looked at all the local schools and the differences between them and not focused on the 'mainstream vs. special' question at all. In the end, doing this is quite a relief because it becomes less about choosing between mainstream and special and more about weighing up the pros and cons of the actual options you have. This also should dispel any myth of selling your child short by not trying mainstream first, because a mainstream education is not an end in itself. Look at the size of the schools and the classes, the teachers and pupils, the ethos and specialities, and so on.

If you have your child's best interests at heart, and you are thoughtful and patient, you are sure to make the right decision.

Choosing a special school

It's first worth stating that the only way to get your child into a special school – with very few exceptions – is for them to have an EHCP. The only exceptions to this would be if parents are self-funding a place at an independent special school or – in very rare cases – if an EHCP is forthcoming but not yet agreed.

If you're looking at special schools for your child, it's worth knowing that special schools do not have to have a SENDCO – SEND truly is everyone's business in special. In such a setting, there may be a range of staff who are well placed to talk to you about their provision, so don't be surprised if the person speaking to you is not a SENDCO.

Some special schools have arrangements that seem at first to be unwelcoming to parents. In the interests of not disrupting the school day for pupils (especially pupils who may be easily unsettled by visitors entering the room), they may say they are unable to give school tours to prospective parents during the school day. They may say they will only give parents a tour if they are named on an EHCP – a frustrating position for parents, who surely want to see a school before their child is enrolled there.

ASKING FOR A CONSULTATION TO BE SENT

In this case, parents can ask for the child's paperwork to be sent to the school via a 'consultation'. Such consultations are sent out by local authorities (it is their duty to do so when parents request it) either while the EHCP is in draft form (i.e., it hasn't yet been finalized) or when it has draft amendments to it (typically following an annual review meeting).

The school will use the paperwork they've been sent to learn a bit about the child and to understand their own appropriateness for your child (Does the child's level of need match their cohort? Do they have the specialist staff required on site, where appropriate?). If they inform the local authority that they do have a place and can meet the needs, that would be the time to make a visit to check if it's what you'd like before proceeding.

When contemplating whether a particular special school is the right one for your child, you might consider the following questions:

WHAT SHOULD I ASK MYSELF... WHEN CONSIDERING A SPECIAL SCHOOL FOR MY CHILD?

Do you like their vision and ethos?

A website will give you an impression, but there's nothing quite like meeting the staff, visiting the school and even chatting with parents whose children already attend the school.

Does their skill and expertise align with the difficulties/differences your child has?

Many special schools are tailored for children with particular needs – autistic pupils, children with profound and multiple learning difficulties, etc.

Does their curriculum offer match your child's potential abilities?

While special schools are typically excellent at offering a personalized curriculum for each child, it's also worth considering whether pupils at the school – or the pupils likely to be in your child's class – are working at a similar level. You'll soon get a sense of this when you ask what the school day looks like, what kind of formal curriculum exists for pupils, etc.

Do they have the specialist therapists on site that your child might need?

Many special schools have a range of therapists working on site – physiotherapists, occupational therapists, SALTs, etc. Their presence on site means that their support is often fully integrated into the teaching – the lines between therapy and teaching are often very positively blurred, with a SALT involved in delivering the English curriculum or a physiotherapist supporting delivery of a PE curriculum, for example.

Choosing an academy or choosing a maintained school

As some parents will know, there are different arrangements for schools in England according to whether a school is an academy or a maintained school. Academies are not under local authority control but are run by an academy trust and are funded by the government. Maintained schools are funded and maintained by the local authority in which they're situated.

However, there is no difference in the legal arrangements for an academy compared with a local-authority-maintained school in relation to admitting pupils with SEND. The same legal arrangements (in relation to admitting a pupil, in relation to non-discriminatory practices) apply.

The impact of a child with SEND attending an academy or a grant-maintained (i.e., non-academy) school is under-researched (Gorard, 2014), but existing research shows no uniform pattern of pupils doing better in one or the other (*ibid.*). Parents will be considering many factors other than academy status – the inclusive nature of the school, its reputation among local parents, the travel time/distance, etc.

Choosing an independent school

There is a slight misconception that when a child has an EHCP, parents can name the school of their choice. While there are elements of truth to this, it often doesn't extend to independent, fee-paying schools.

A local authority has a duty to provide an education that meets a child's needs. Getting a place for your child at some independent schools requires you, the parent, to prove that other schools (i.e., the special school that the local authority already commissions places for rather than an independent alternative) could not meet your child's needs.

The complexity here is that for some schools – those called 'Section 41 schools' – their legal status in this regard is slightly different. Rather than go through the complexities here, we will recommend IPSEA's work in this area, and their webpage 'Section 41 schools/colleges'.

Section 41 schools/colleges, (IPSEA) Independent Provider of Special Education Advice

www.ipsea.org.uk/FAQs/section-41-schools-colleges

Choosing a school if the current school placement has broken down

What parents want is typically very reasonable: regular enough contact, an understanding of what happens during the child's school day and confidence that the school makes good choices if/when things aren't going so well for their child.

Though the time of school staff is typically incredibly pressured, the most successful schools ensure they have systems so that these reasonable parent requests can be met.

FINDING OUT ABOUT SCHOOLS IN YOUR AREA

When you feel that a school placement is beyond repair, you might be looking locally to see what other provisions exist. You might look at a 'Local Offer' website (see page 89); you might contact your nearest SENDIASS (see page 215); you might tap into local networks of parents whose children have SEND. All of these sources should contain a wealth of knowledge about local school options.

REQUESTING A CHANGE OF SCHOOL

If the answer lies in a change of school placement, there are a number of ways to do this. The method primarily depends on whether or not your child has an EHCP:

CHILDREN RECEIVING 'SEN SUPPORT'

If your child doesn't have an EHCP, you will be subject to your local authority's admissions arrangements; you will go through the same process as a parent of a child with no SEND.

Find out the process involved for 'in-year admissions' where you live by looking at the schools section of your local authority's website.

If you do want your child to start in a particular school, that school cannot legally refuse your child because they have SEND (it is slightly different if they have an EHCP, see below). There may be other valid reasons – your distance from the school, a lack of available space in a given year group, etc. – for them not to enrol your child.

CHILDREN WITH AN EHCP

If your child does have an EHCP and you want them to go to a different school, you need to ask the current school and/or your local authority for an 'early annual review'. This will mean that your annual review meeting (see page 99 for more on annual reviews) is held without you having to wait a whole year.

At this early annual review meeting, you will have the chance to share the name of the school(s) you are considering for your child. You will then ask the local authority to 'consult' these schools. They will send your child's paperwork (the EHCP, supporting advice, recent annual review paperwork, etc.) out to those schools; the schools will have 15 calendar days to respond.

If you would like more details about the different types of schools available, the excellent IPSEA website has a useful section on this for parents:

IPSEA – Types of Schools and Other Settings
www.ipsea.org.uk/types-of-schools-and-other-settings

Legal rights around school choice

In terms of your legal rights as a parent, there are some differences here, based on whether or not your child has an EHCP.

Requesting a setting for a child who has SEND but no EHCP

The first thing to be clear about is that a mainstream school cannot refuse to admit a child on the grounds of them having SEND. For a child receiving 'SEN Support' (i.e., who does not have an EHCP), this means that normal admissions processes apply – if your child has a right to a place in that school through their admissions criteria (based on having a sibling in the school already or living near the school, etc.), they cannot be denied a place because they have additional needs of some kind.

That said, if the school is full, there is no requirement for that school to go over its pupil numbers in a given year group in order to admit your child.

As mentioned above, special schools are almost universally for pupils with an EHCP. Any route for your child to go to a special school is likely to first require them to obtain an EHCP. That said, if urgent specialist placement is required and an EHCP is not yet in place – for example, if you have recently moved to the country – you should contact your local authority SEND department to ascertain how they can support your child to obtain appropriate educational provision as soon as possible.

Requesting a setting for a child with an EHCP

Where your child has an EHCP, there is a bit more to the process. As a parent, the current process is that you are asked to name a placement that you'd like to receive a consultation (i.e., the local authority will send your child's paperwork to the school(s) of your choice and ask them to consider how they might meet the needs of your child).

Parents have a right to ask for almost any school to be consulted. Local authorities have a duty to consult these schools unless such a school is wholly independent (at which point the local authority could choose whether or not to consult). You might choose schools: that are mainstream *and* special; that are in the local authority you live in, as well as other local authorities; that may be a mix of academies and local-authority-maintained schools; that have a Specialist Resource Provision (see page 87); etc.

The local authority will send all the schools you wish to receive this consultation the relevant paperwork (EHCP, etc.), after which the schools have 15 days to respond (to the local authority rather than to you) about next steps.

Those next steps might be:

- the school would love to admit your child
- the school has concerns about their ability to admit your child.

When a school believes they shouldn't admit your child

When your child has an EHCP, and a school has received their paperwork as a consultation from the local authority, a school might refer to one of three legal arguments to state why they don't believe they can offer your child a place:

- The setting is unsuitable for the age, ability, aptitude or SEN of the child or young person.
- The attendance of the child or young person would be incompatible with the provision of efficient education for others.
- The attendance of the child or young person would be incompatible with the efficient use of resources.

Although the school might make one of these arguments, it is then the local authority that will make the decision here about whether the school's argument is one it can legally agree with.

Note that a school being full is not a legally binding reason not to admit your child if they have an EHCP. Though this can create very real challenges for schools (there are only so many desks in a classroom, only so many pupils who can access the sensory room, etc.), the law is largely on the side of parents here.

In a scenario where you have chosen the school you'd like your child (with an EHCP) to go to but they have responded with 'no', that is not the end of the road. The local authority will still be required to name the school unless it can demonstrate that one of the three legally binding justifications is true for your child. Let's take each of those in turn:

THE SETTING IS UNSUITABLE FOR THE AGE, ABILITY, APTITUDE OR SEN OF THE CHILD OR YOUNG PERSON

Though schools have the right to make this argument, in the case of a mainstream school, this legal right is trumped by a parent's legal right to a mainstream education for their child. To be clear: the legal right for parents to have a mainstream education for their child is stronger than the school's right to say their school is unsuitable on the grounds stated above.

In the case of a request for a special school, the local authority would often be investigating whether the child's needs are *not significant enough* for a specialist setting (i.e., the needs could be met in mainstream). If the local authority chooses not to name a specialist setting, even when parents want it, the local authority will need to prove that the needs are not great enough and/or that one of the other reasons above applies.

THE ATTENDANCE OF THE CHILD OR YOUNG PERSON WOULD BE INCOMPATIBLE WITH THE PROVISION OF EFFICIENT EDUCATION FOR OTHERS

This might mean that the school is saying your child will prevent others from learning, potentially for a number of different reasons (e.g., they believe their behaviour will disrupt others' learning).

In the case of a mainstream school, if they believe a particular child with an EHCP may have an impact upon 'the provision of efficient education for others', there is an additional requirement: the school and the local authority would need to show that there are no 'reasonable steps' they could take to prevent that incompatibility. The legal bar is high in terms of these 'reasonable steps' – i.e., the school and local authority would be expected to go a long way towards adjusting and providing additional provision rather than simply saying that a child cannot attend.

THE ATTENDANCE OF THE CHILD OR YOUNG PERSON WOULD BE INCOMPATIBLE WITH THE EFFICIENT USE OF RESOURCES

In terms of incompatibility with the 'efficient use of resources', a school might make this argument if they would need to install a lift or make other significant structural changes to a school building to meet your child's needs. Transport costs are one of the most common reasons for a local authority to say a school will be incompatible with the efficient use of resources, for example, if parents have chosen a school that is slightly further away.

If the local authority sides with the school here (rather than you as the parent), it will have to show that the extra cost is significant or disproportionate.

Annual reviews

If your child already has an EHCP, you'll be familiar with the term 'annual review'. Part of a local authority's statutory duty around EHCPs is to review them annually to ensure they remain relevant, accurate and appropriate to the child's current needs. This process includes a meeting (typically called an 'annual review' or 'annual review meeting'). Note that where a child is under five, local authorities 'should consider' having these meetings more than annually.

In practice, the duty to arrange an 'annual review' meeting is often delegated to the school, which should ensure that information is gathered, a meeting is organized, views are heard and paperwork is submitted.

Before the annual review meeting

At least two weeks before it happens, you should be invited to attend an 'annual review' meeting, which will typically take place at your child's school. Someone at the school – typically the SENDCO – must invite anyone who is relevant to your child's provision across education, health and social care, including the local authority (though in practice, many local authorities will only attend a select few annual review meetings – e.g., perhaps those where the child's EHCP needs substantial amendments). Parents should be central to the process of annual review – the views of parents and children are paramount here.

The SENDCO will also request any new advice before the annual review meeting. This will typically mean inviting you and relevant adults to feed back on the progress your child has made within the last year. It may also mean asking external professionals (therapists or specialist teachers working with your child, etc.) to conduct fresh assessments and/or provide an update on the child's needs, the progress made, new 'outcomes', etc.

Any new advice or information should be circulated to all parties at least two weeks before the annual review meeting.

During the annual review meeting

Typically, the SENDCO will share the progress made by the child in school and will invite others to share the progress of the child from their perspective.

During the meeting, it is vital that you and your child have the chance to share your views. You might already have considered whether you'd like that to happen spontaneously within the meeting, whether you'd like a friend to speak on your behalf, whether you'd rather provide something in writing in advance, etc. Likewise, you or the school may have gathered your child's views before the meeting (by video, through a 'Talking Mat' – see page 187, etc.), or they might voice their own views during all or part of the meeting.

Though it's not always necessary to review every line of the EHCP within the meeting, the discussion would be expected to cover the continued accuracy of the needs listed in the EHCP, the progress made (particularly towards the EHCP 'outcomes') and the appropriateness of the provision in place to help meet those outcomes.

Other sections may also be important. As a parent, it may be helpful for you to go to the meeting with a clear idea of any lines/sections of the EHCP that you'd like discussed and/or amended.

WHAT SHOULD I ASK... DURING AN ANNUAL REVIEW MEETING?

- What updated advice have you received for this annual review?
- What progress is my child making in school?
- Are the needs listed in the EHCP still accurate, in your opinion?
- Do you believe changes need to be made to the provision that is in place for my child?
- Do you believe my child is making good progress towards their outcomes?

As stated above, parents should not merely be asking questions in an annual review – they should also be answering them! The views of families in relation to the questions above (and beyond) are essential.

After the annual review meeting

Following the annual review meeting, the paperwork will be sent off (by the SENDCO, typically) to all attendees, and to the local authority, within two weeks.

The local authority then has four weeks in which to decide to:

- maintain the EHCP without any changes
- amend the EHCP
- cease the EHCP.

Parents have the right to appeal where they are not happy with the local authority's actions.

When a local authority concludes an annual review by proposing to amend an EHCP, it must also notify you of the proposed amendments within four weeks of the meeting. The final EHCP must be issued as soon as practicable and within a further eight weeks.

Local authorities must inform you about how an appeal can be made; you can expect them to do this in writing when telling you about their decision (i.e., their decision to amend or to cease the EHCP). If you wish to appeal the amendments being made to a plan, the right of appeal will only come when the final amended plan is issued.

Transition points

If you want to learn more about how you might choose a school for your child, see page 85. When they do come to change nursery or school provision, it can be unsettling for a child; it can also represent excitement, progress and positive change. That said, such transitions are almost always the cause of some anxiety for parents, particularly if their child has SEND.

Where your child has an EHCP, that transfers with them from

one setting to the next. There is no need for a new application, and the EHCP doesn't cease just because the child is changing schools. Although the school's voice is heard here in relation to whether or not they can meet the child's needs, parents have a strong legal right to the provision they request for their child (see page 96).

In many cases, parents will experience a transition process that is thorough, is personalized and leaves no room for surprises. After all, it is in the best interests of the new school to understand their new pupils as extensively as possible before they arrive.

Understanding the transition process

If you're not sure how thoroughly or successfully this transition is being supported, you might ask the following when your child is approaching a change of school:

WHAT SHOULD I ASK... WHEN MY CHILD IS CHANGING SCHOOL?

Questions for the school they are leaving

- How are you preparing my child for their upcoming change?
- What information will you transfer to the new school and when will you be doing so?
- How are you communicating with the new school about my child's needs?

Questions for the school they are joining

- How will you make sure you understand my child's needs before they start with you? What role can I play in that as their parent?
- What opportunities are you providing for my child to learn about your school before they start (through visits, through appropriately targeted written communication, etc.)?
- What kind of support do you see yourselves providing when my child starts at your school?

At home, you might consider finding opportunities to make the transition feel real for your child. Depending on your child's age and level of understanding, this might mean making your own social story about the new school (see page 137), practising the journey with your child or reading books together about how we sometimes feel when things change.

There is no one perfect transition programme. You'll want to get a sense that preparation will start well in advance, that both settings are in communication with one another and that your child's needs and views, as well as yours as a parent, are at the heart of the transition process.

PRIMARY TO SECONDARY TRANSITION – THE VIEW FROM A SECONDARY SENDCO

Michelle offers some advice for families approaching primary to secondary transition for their child.

One of the most important things we can do as SENDCOs is to work together with parents and carers. Never is this more true than during the process of transition.

When you have decided on a secondary school that you think will support your child, contact the SENDCO and ask how they can support a smooth transition. It is helpful for us to have a really informed and up-to-date profile of students, including an accurate picture of the level of need. Let us know about any interventions and support your child had, what worked and what didn't. Think about what worked at primary school and how we can try to bring that into secondary school.

Our need to learn from parents

The support offered at secondary school will often look a bit different, because there can be a greater focus on preparing our students for independence. For example, teaching assistants may not work one-to-one with students in quite the same way as in some primary schools. This is a big change for some families. We therefore really value open and honest dialogue with parents.

Helping us to get it right

If something is not working, tell us. Our role as SENDCOs in school is to ensure that everyone in the school is supporting students with additional needs, but sometimes things do go wrong.

When this happens, we want to fix it and we want to work with you to find solutions. Please do share suggestions, if you have them, of how we can better support your child in school.

Remember that your voice is important – you know your child best and you know what works.

Michelle Copeland, Secondary SENDCO

Transitioning to higher education

In the majority of cases, if a young person enters higher education, the local authority is no longer responsible for their education – the EHCP will cease. That said, your child still has the statutory protection outlined within the Equality Act (2010); a university is still duty-bound to value the young person's 'protected characteristic' if they have a disability. For the young person, accessing the right support will be about working closely with the university to understand how their needs can best be met without an EHCP. See the 'Higher education' section on page 121 for more details on how a university might support a young person with SEND.

Funding for pupils with SEND

When the system works well, parents should not have to worry too much about sources or amounts of funding (do any of us know how much the support from a GP costs each year?!). However, there may be times when it feels like every penny needs to be fought for. Having a basic understanding of school funding within this area may therefore feel helpful.

School funding for all pupils

All providers of state-funded, statutory education in England receive money from the government in order to run. Once a child is in statutory education, from Reception onwards in England, the school will also receive a set amount of funding ('Age-Weighted Pupil Unit' funding) to meet the needs of every child on their roll.

In addition, each local authority sets its own formula – typically factoring in deprivation, English as an Additional Language and prior attainment – to distribute an 'SEN Notional Budget' to schools and academies. This money provides some additional provision for pupils who have (or may have) SEND. This money is not ring-fenced and is not attributed to individual children as such.

High-needs funding

In addition to the SEN Notional Budget, the school will be given high-needs funding for some pupils; typically, those who have an EHCP (though some local authorities issue EHCPs that come with no additional funding,[5] while other local authorities have ways of accessing high-needs funding without an EHCP). It is typically expected – though without a legal basis to support it – that schools will spend up to £6000 of their SEN Notional Budget per year on meeting an individual child's needs before being able to access high-needs funding.

Banding

If your child has an EHCP, you may have heard about 'Banding'. This is the term typically used to describe the assigning of a particular level of funding to a particular child based on the accepted levels of provision required. Using the needs outlined in the EHCP as the basis, the local authority will decide the level of 'Banding' (or funding) required in order for that child to have their needs met.

Attendance to school

The average percentage attendance of pupils to school has dropped since the COVID-19 pandemic, both for pupils with SEND and for pupils with no SEND. For some disabled pupils, medical appointments or health complications can create an additional barrier to attending school regularly.

There is no legal allowance for a pupil with SEND to have lower

---

5   The local authority is responsible for securing the special educational provision in Section F of an EHCP, regardless of funding arrangements.

attendance than a student without SEND. Children have an entitlement to receive a full-time education, and schools have a duty to deliver this; this extends to all pupils, irrespective of need. This ordinarily relies on the child being physically in school.

That said, there may be valid reasons why a specific child's health needs (including mental health needs) or individual circumstances affect their attendance. There may be valid reasons why a child's 65% attendance should be acknowledged by the school to be the best that is possible at that stage.

Attendance is perhaps the greatest area where ongoing positive communication and partnership between school and home is beneficial.

It is helpful when parents appreciate the duty on schools to provide a full-time education for pupils, which typically starts by pupils attending regularly.

It is vital though that schools also appreciate the very real difficulties in and differences to family life when a child in the family has SEND and consider what implications this might have for school attendance.

A spirit of positive cooperation towards a common aim is where the best work happens. A respectful and open dialogue between school and home goes a long way towards helping to ensure the child makes it into school.

For more on attendance, see the 'School avoidance' section below (page 112).

Addressing difficulties your child is having at school

You will know instinctively if your child is happy and positive about their experience at school. You will see how they are the night before school, on the way to school and when Grandma asks them how they're enjoying Year 1.

When your child is neither happy nor positive, it's important to feel confident about how to work through issues in positive partnership with the school. Where difficulties arise, the relationship you have with the school can be key to unlocking any difficulties and implementing effective solutions.

EFFECTIVE SCHOOL–PARENT PARTNERSHIP

Gary shares his own experience of working with schools on developing healthy and positive relationships with families.

You will undoubtedly want the relationship you have with your child's school to be a healthy and positive one. This will be a shared aim – I've never met a school that didn't want healthy and positive relationships with families, even if the way some of them did this, or the time they were able to dedicate to it, didn't always make this shared aim obvious.

When working with any school colleague around SEND (especially when something isn't going well for a child), I encourage colleagues to remain calm, to start each day afresh and to ensure all involved are treated with dignity. I discourage schools from going straight for 'we can't meet their needs', and instead encourage colleagues to be considered, rational and solution-focused in their support for children and in their partnership work with parents.

As long as a school is taking this approach, it is always helpful if parents can pinpoint (if possible) what the issue is and be willing to listen to potential compromises – within limits – that can support their child to be successful; how can your child's needs be met (and statutory entitlements delivered) while also placing realistic demands upon school staff?

The school's position

Though you know your child better than anyone else can, it is also true that teachers know teaching best and understand their classroom best, and that their views on a way forward can often be insightful and practicable. They might have a view, for example, on whether a change in the seating plan or a different lunchtime arrangement could be unhelpful at this stage; if so, they should be willing to explain to you why they feel this is the case.

There may be times when the school tells you that your child appears happy and is making good progress, but this doesn't match what you see at home or believe to be the case. The school could be wrong – the child could be masking a difficulty (see glossary) – but it could be that they are right, and your child is anxious about things that they can be reassured about. In this case, your work with your child may be about helping them to see the positives and offering reassurance about school rather than necessarily needing the school to make changes to their provision for your child.

Open communication

As with so many things, effective two-way communication between the school and parents is essential, often even more so where a child has SEND. Where school isn't going wonderfully for your child, good communication between home and school staff can sometimes be half the battle in the bid for positive change. Regular communication can help you to remain aware of the provision that is currently in place for your child, to know when the child's current support is due to be reviewed and to understand what the potential options are if the support needs to be increased/changed. Regular communication can help the school to know what your child is saying about being in class, whether they slept well last night and/or that they have a new special interest.

This regular communication might look like a home–school communication book, a conversation at the gate and/or booking in semi-regular meetings throughout the year. You might choose to speak to your child's class teacher or the school SENDCO if you think communication methods need to be addressed or communication needs to increase.

WHAT SHOULD I ASK... WHEN THE COMMUNICATION ISN'T RIGHT?

- Who is my main point of contact at the school?
- What communication can I realistically expect to have with the school?
- How can we make sure our communication is two-way?
- How can I let you know if something at home might affect them in school (e.g., a poor night's sleep)?
- How and when will we review my child's progress and provision throughout the year?

Problems with peers

It's unfortunately true that some pupils with SEND can become the victims of bullying – one study put this at 37% of pupils (Department for Education, 2019). There will be huge variation within this number of course, with many schools creating the kind of nurturing and accepting environment that results in very little bullying behaviour.

However, every parent worries that their child will have difficulties with their peers. If your child is pre-verbal or merely chooses (on some level) not to communicate with you about school, you can feel totally at sea with what's going on and how to move forward.

If it's clear that your child is having difficulties with a peer or group of peers, the starting point will usually be the adult who knows your child best – their teacher, the SENDCO or perhaps a teaching assistant. It's important for children to know that difficulties with peers don't always equate to bullying but also that bullying is never something that a child should have to tolerate.

A conversation with school about such difficulties might mean asking some of the following questions:

WHAT SHOULD I ASK... WHEN MY CHILD HAS PROBLEMS WITH THEIR PEERS?

- Have you noticed my child having difficulties with any other children?
- Can you monitor my child's peer relationships and give me feedback after a day/week (as appropriate)?
- Are you developing a plan to either support my child, educate (or, where needed, sanction) other children and/ or separate pupils?
- When can we meet again to review how things are going?

Concerns from the school's side

It may be that your child's school is raising difficulties with you. In most cases, these are often more minor in nature, with the school telling you that your child has 'had a difficult day' or similar. In the most significant and much rarer cases, they may tell you that theirs is not the right setting for your child.

'THEY'VE HAD A DIFFICULT DAY'

Parents have many responses when being told this news. Some will be grateful to know about it so they can try and address it in some way at home. Some will understandably feel defensive of their child and want to challenge the school about what the school staff did in response (or perhaps in the run-up) to something happening. Others may feel at a loss – perhaps they are the only parent being spoken to at the school gates about their child's 'difficult day'. Some parents may feel all of these emotions at once.

It is hard to know what to do as a parent when this happens. Sometimes, speaking to a child about their day in the evening, when they may be calm and regulated, is a perfect opportunity for reflection and for the parent to get a full grasp of what happened and why. At other times, rehashing the day's events can be distressing for a child and does not help them to move forward at all. Your knowledge of your child (and perhaps some trial and error) will be your guide on this one.

As a parent, you must never undervalue your own knowledge of your child. When a teacher is trying to interpret the underlying cause of a particular behaviour being shown by your child in school, you may well hold the vital piece of the puzzle that can help the school work out what is going wrong. Your understanding of a peer falling-out, a sensory trigger or a difficulty in manipulating numbers might be just the jigsaw piece the school is looking for.

One thing you will want to do, of course, is to work with the school to try and make the next day better. As well as sharing your own views (and perhaps your child's views) on what happened or what they need, you might also ask any of the following questions:

WHAT SHOULD I ASK... WHEN MY CHILD'S 'HAD A DIFFICULT DAY'?

- Are we both communicating enough with each other about how they are at home/at school?

- Do you think there is something that caused them to have a harder day today?
- What discussion would you like me to have with them about today?
- How are you adapting your support so that they have a less difficult day tomorrow?

'THIS MAY NOT BE THE SCHOOL FOR YOUR CHILD'

You may find yourself hearing these words at some point in your child's school career.

First, it's worth acknowledging the difficulty in hearing this as a parent. If you've put your faith in a school and they are saying it's not working, that can have a significant impact on you as a parent. It can make parents feel guilty for not having had a crystal ball to predict such an outcome.

Second, it's worth listening to what the school's concerns are. It's possible the school doesn't currently have the understanding they need of your child, the training they need to educate your child or the resources in order to deliver effective provision to your child. These may all be problems that have solutions. In your discussions with the school, make sure they have considered these as challenges that can be met.

Legally, any school will need to be making 'reasonable adjustments' for a child with a disability, and most schools must be using 'best endeavours' to meet the needs of a child with SEN. They both equate to the same thing – a commitment that work needs to be done to accommodate and support your child when they have additional needs.

For a child with no EHCP, it's not as simple as a school saying they can't meet your child's needs – it would be unlawful for them to 'off-roll' your child for this reason. If your child's behaviour is a serious breach of the school's behaviour policy, the school may push for a permanent exclusion, but parents have full right to appeal if this is the course of action being taken by the school.

For a child with an EHCP, the school may call an early annual review (see page 95), during which they might put it to you (and to the local authority) that they can no longer meet the needs of the child. This isn't the end of it though – remember the strong legal right to mainstream education set out in the Children and Families Act (2014) (see page 72). Even if a school is stating that they can no longer meet the needs of your child, this position is trumped in law by parental preference for a certain school. If you feel your legal right is being discounted in this regard, you might seek support from your local SENDIASS, phone the SOS!SEN service or look at the IPSEA website for further advice and support.

SOS!SEN – free national SEND helpline for parents
www.sossen.org.uk/services/helpline

If, however, you are also looking for a change of school for your child, look at page 95 for information on how you might go about this.

School avoidance

For some pupils, the thought of going to school can induce significant anxiety, which leads to them not attending. Across much of the country, this has come to be known as Emotionally Based School Avoidance, or EBSA.

The excellent Young Minds website (www.youngminds.org.uk) has a page for parents who are struggling to get their children into school (Young Minds, n.d.). It explores anxiety in young people before looking at strategies to try at home, conversations that could be had with the school and ways to approach a total refusal to attend. Young Minds recommends some strategies you can try at home, such as 'Create a morning routine or timetable,' 'Think together about how your child can manage their anxiety' and 'Encourage them to do things that help them relax' (Young Minds, 2022).

Where too often discussions become about sanctions for children and fines for parents, there is also much excellent work that takes place when a child is struggling to attend school.

The most effective work in supporting children back into school starts early, involves partnership between family and school and is solution-focused, with the child at the heart of discussions. It involves the school, family and young person trying to identify answers to some of the following questions:

WHAT SHOULD I ASK... WHEN MY CHILD IS AVOIDING SCHOOL?

Because of the collaborative approach required where school avoidance is present, these questions are written in a spirit of total collaboration. You'll see 'we' rather than 'you' in these questions. You'll also see some example answers on the right-hand side.

Do we know what the **root cause** of the school avoidance is? What is the worry?	For example, the noise in the lunch hall, the size of the older pupils, the volume of the teacher's voice when they're cross or the act of separating from parents at the school gates.
Can we do anything to **rationalize** the worry?	For example, the pupil could be taught that older pupils don't need to be feared, perhaps through a peer mentoring programme (or just through being introduced to some of these pupils).
Can we do anything to **remove the cause** of the worry?	For example, the child could go to the front of the lunch queue so they avoid the height of the noise or they could bring a comforting item from home into the classroom with them to support the transition to school in the morning.
Can we do anything to **incentivize** attendance?	For example, the school might make sure that the child has a motivating activity they do in school with an adult each day.
Can we do anything to ensure the child feels **listened to and supported** if they do feel worried when at school?	For example, the child could be shown whom they can speak to and/or how they can appropriately ask for help when they need it. A non-verbal system of doing this can be implemented where helpful.

USING DETECTIVE WORK
Stephen describes working with his son's school when he stopped wanting to attend.

When our son started Reception at his special school, everything went okay. He was excited about his smart new uniform and the school had a tried-and-tested method for helping young children to settle into their new environment.

After a few weeks, however, things changed. Suddenly, it was a real effort to get him ready in the morning and he expressed clearly (through his behaviour) that he didn't want to go. We still managed to get him through the gate in the morning, but it was clear something wasn't right.

Because he had very little language, he wasn't able to explain what was upsetting him. Luckily, his school is very open and the teachers are always available to talk to. I chatted to his teacher at the school gate and later on the phone too. We figured out the day his attitude towards school had changed and thought through what could be the cause.

After toing and froing, we figured out it was something to do with lunchtime. By a process of elimination, we didn't think it was the food or the noise of the lunchroom. And then his teacher remembered that – except for the day he was upset – he had always sat in the same seat. It turns out he was distressed because, having just about gotten used to everything that was new about his routine, someone had gone and thrown in a big heap of uncertainty by sitting in his usual chair.

The school was great and agreed to reserve him the same seat every day from then on. They even put a special cushion on it so he and the other children knew it was his. Quite quickly some of his anxiety subsided and things got back to normal.

School trips

Attending school trips is part of the richness of being a school pupil. They provide pupils with what schools often call 'cultural capital'; they can help to teach important life skills and to foster pupil independence. For pupils with SEND, this is no less true.

The primary concern of any school should be (and, in our experience, always is) the safety of pupils. Risk assessments are standard practice for school trips so that any safety issues can be considered; it is expected that pupils' needs will be factored into the risk assessment process.

However, children with SEND have a legal right to be involved in the activities of the school; schools 'must secure that the child engages in the activities of the school together with children who do not have special educational needs' (Children and Families Act, 2014).

There are exceptions of course, which are also set out in the Children and Families Act (2014) and which have been summarized by IPSEA, below:

The school can only exclude them from activities if:

- it is not reasonably practicable for them to be included
- being included would prevent them from receiving the support they need
- being included would prevent the efficient education of other children or the efficient use of resources.

IPSEA (n.d.(b))

The school's role therefore is to make decisions that have both inclusion and pupil safety in mind, in line with the legal framework set out above.

Residential trips

BUT ARE THEY READY?

Gary shares his own experience of working with families around their child attending a residential trip.

I've experienced cases where a child with SEND was just not ready to attend a residential trip with their school. However, I've also experienced many more cases where a child with SEND has thrived on a residential trip, even where there have been significant barriers to overcome to make that happen.

In those latter cases, working with families was absolutely crucial. It was also crucial that we both shared two principles here: that the child's safety and wellbeing was absolutely essential, and that the inclusion of the child in activities with their peers was highly desirable and what we should therefore be aiming for wherever possible.

What this then looked like in practice was different in each case but sometimes included meetings with the parents way in advance of the trip, looking at webpages of the trip organizer or meeting with the trip organizer directly, preparing social stories for the parent to read with their child at home or preparing contingency plans in case the trip doesn't go as planned.

I found there was no magic formula for this – as with so many things, it goes right when staff and parents communicate well and with respect for each other, and when a child's safety and inclusion run as key principles from both parties.

As a parent, you will wish to get a bit of extra information about the trip before agreeing for your child to go. You might find yourself contributing substantially to the planning or even, in rarer cases, attending the trip alongside your child. That might mean asking any of the following questions:

WHAT SHOULD I ASK... WHEN MY CHILD IS ATTENDING A RESIDENTIAL TRIP?

- How will activities be adapted so that my child's needs can be met?
- Do you have specific concerns about their safety? If so, how are you planning to overcome these concerns?
- Which elements of the support they normally receive will take place while they're away? Which other aspects of support will they receive?
- What work will you do before the trip in order to prepare my child for the trip? How can I support this at home?
- Which adults are attending the trip? Will someone be there who has a good understanding of my child's needs?

> - How (and how often) will you communicate with me as a parent during the trip?
> - What is the contingency plan for if things are not working out?

By knowing the answers to these questions, you can be confident that your child's needs have been acknowledged and their safety and wellbeing are at the forefront of the school's planning.

Life in secondary school

There are typical rites of passage in secondary schools. It's worth thinking about a few of these in relation to pupils with SEND:

Year 9 'options'

Typically undertaken in Year 9, though sometimes in Year 8, this describes the process by which pupils choose the subjects they will study in Years 10 and 11, typically through GCSE qualifications. It should be an exciting time in which pupils have the chance to do more of the subjects they enjoy at the expense of those they perhaps don't.

A few things are worth understanding in relation to SEND:

SCHOOLS ARE UNDER PRESSURE

That pressure is real and can affect things like Ofsted judgements. Schools may look to enrol your child on more courses than you think is sensible or on a more academic pathway than you think is realistic.

DIFFERENT SCHOOLS MAY OFFER SLIGHTLY DIFFERENT COURSES

If a school doesn't run Food Technology, and only your child wants to study it, there may be no solution to this – in most cases, a school is unlikely to be able to change its curriculum offer for one child.

THERE ARE DIFFERENT COURSES OUT THERE

Schools may well look to enrol all pupils on 'Level 2' (i.e., a GCSE pass) courses. However, there are also 'Entry Level' and 'Level 1' courses that allow pupils to learn and get qualified at what might be a more realistic level for them.

Typically, children with SEND will go through this process slightly differently to their peers. Your child might complete their options 'form' together with the SENDCO, or there might be a tailored offer for them that gives priority access to certain types of course (e.g., 'Functional Skills' courses) due to their SEND.

As a parent, the school should make time to speak to you if you have concerns about this process. If the school goes down a road you're not entirely happy with, work out with the school when it can be reviewed, and what could potentially change as a result.

Work experience

This can be very useful for pupils. It can help them to appreciate an element of adulthood that they hadn't quite understood; it can help them to value the importance of work; it can even help to motivate them in their studies. It's important that all pupils prepare for adulthood by having some exposure to the workplace while they are in school.

That said, spending a week in an unfamiliar environment, with adults who don't know them and with a new and unwritten set of expectations, can be tricky for some children with SEND.

You should therefore be working with the school on what a good halfway house might look like. Options could include the following:

SUPPORTED WORK EXPERIENCE

Either through your school or through a scheme run by your local authority, supported work experience placements may well be available. These would typically involve working with employers who have some understanding of neurodivergence, who take the time to get to know your child before they begin their work experience and who understand that a successful placement might look a little different to that of other pupils.

USING YOUR OWN NETWORKS

Many schools will be delighted if you organize the work experience placement for your child. This might mean they spend some time at the family business, in the workplace of a neighbour or helping out a family friend. The presence of a familiar adult may provide a less realistic experience of work, but it may also give your child the head start that allows for a successful placement.

Joining the sixth form

During Year 11, pupils (and their families) typically make a choice about where to complete post-16 study, whether within the current school, through another school or by attending college. Many schools offer rather narrow options at sixth form, delivering only A level courses, for which GCSEs at Grades 6 and above may be needed.

While A level courses will be appropriate for many pupils with SEND, they require an academic demand that makes them unrealistic for some pupils. Even if the young person has the protection of an EHCP, there is little point in keeping a child in a setting where the courses on offer are ones that they are highly likely to struggle to access.

If your child is in Year 11, it is worth finding out early what the sixth form offer is and whether or not your child is on course to reach the grades that make joining the sixth form appropriate/possible. If not, you may want to explore local colleges and other sixth forms, perhaps by asking local networks and/or by looking at your authority's Local Offer.

You will want to attend an open evening; these are normally held during the autumn term for the following September's enrolment. When going around the school/college, you might ask the following questions:

WHAT SHOULD I ASK... AT A SCHOOL/ COLLEGE SIXTH FORM OPEN EVENING?

- What support do you provide for pupils with SEND?
- What grades are required in order for a pupil to attend here?
- How do you support a pupil if they don't attain a pass grade at GCSE?
- How do you prepare young people for adulthood, particularly when they have SEND?
- What co-curricular opportunities do you offer? How do you ensure these are inclusive of pupils with SEND?

Life after secondary school

Some parents – not all, admittedly – have excellent relationships with their child's school. They feel confident in the staff's deep understanding and genuine love for their child and feel calm about the school's ability to get many situations right and to reflect/engage with them when they get something wrong.

Losing this feeling can be quite nervy. Though your child may be approaching adulthood (whether at 16, 18 or 19), many young people lack the skills required to exist in an adult world, including self-advocacy.

Support needn't end when your child leaves school. Whatever their next steps, their needs will go with them, and so must their support. This looks a little different depending on the setting.

Further education colleges

Typically, further education colleges will offer a wide range of courses, catering for pupils across the attainment range. As such, they will be teaching courses that may be practical and vocational, with learning support departments that support access for pupils who still need it.

Crucially, EHCPs can last until the end of the academic year in which a young person has turned 25. Although the way support is delivered in a college setting may be different to how it is delivered within a school setting, the college will still use their 'best endeavours' to deliver the provision stated in Section F of the EHCP.

Whether or not your child has an EHCP, your experience as a parent may not change enormously when your child moves from school to college. Of course, as your child approaches adulthood, you will want (and typically expect) your child to have more direct involvement in decisions about the support they will receive. Nevertheless, as a parent, you can still look to be a partner in the provision delivered, have two-way communication with the college and be updated about your child's progress.

Higher education

EHCPs typically end if a young person enrols in a course at a higher education institution such as a university. However, the young person's right to support does not end. Disability is a legally protected characteristic, and all universities have a duty to ensure students are not put at a substantial disadvantage because of their disability.

If your child is looking to apply to a university, make it part of your research to understand what kind of support is available from their learning support department. This might include equipment, academic support and/or tailored accommodation.

The following page of the UCAS website outlines how disabled people applying for university might navigate the system so that their needs can still be understood, considered and met:

UCAS – Students with Physical or Mental Health Conditions and Learning Differences

www.ucas.com/undergraduate/applying-university/individual-needs/disabled-students

---

Support for disabled students at university can be funded via a Disabled Students' Allowance, about which more information can be found here:

Disabled Students' Allowance

www.gov.uk/disabled-students-allowance-dsa

The world of work

Though employers don't have SEND registers and EHCPs in the same way schools do, a disabled young person entering the world of work is protected by the Equality Act (2010).

It is against the law to treat someone less favourably than someone else because of a personal characteristic such as religion, sex, gender reassignment or age.

Discrimination can include:

- not hiring someone
- selecting a particular person for redundancy

- paying someone less than another worker without good reason.

You can discriminate against someone even if you do not intend to. For example, you can discriminate indirectly by offering working conditions or rules that disadvantage one group of people more than another.

UK Government (n.d.(a))

Support while in the workplace

Financial support is available for disabled people in the workplace, via the government's Access to Work scheme:

Access to Work can help you get or stay in work if you have a physical or mental health condition or disability.
The support you get will depend on your needs. Through Access to Work, you can apply for:

- a grant to help pay for practical support with your work
- support with managing your mental health at work
- money to pay for communication support at job interviews.

UK Government (n.d.(b))

Although many readers of this book will have children who are in early childhood rather than approaching adulthood, the protections above may offer some reassurance when considering what the future holds for your child. The right to equality is a lifelong one, and there are mechanisms in place to try and deliver and fund this in reality.

That said, it would be misleading to suggest that these mechanisms work smoothly for disabled people all the time. Data around employability – amongst many other forms of data in relation to the lives of disabled adults – suggests that the system still doesn't consistently offer high-quality support and still doesn't deliver equal access for disabled people in relation to the world of work.

CHAPTER 3

SUPPORTING YOUR CHILD'S LEARNING

The best people to know how to interact with a child are their parents. Parents often know, sometimes with no language needed, how their child truly feels or what they're trying to communicate – what they really mean or what they truly need.

This chapter includes information about how to support your child's schoolwork and how to help them learn general life skills. These are some of the most common and most effective techniques you can employ. They are also, very intentionally, the simplest; and once you understand the principles behind each one, you can use them for whatever difficulties you and your child face. Social stories (page 137) will often work as well for road safety as they do for explaining why you have to wear a school uniform. Visual timetables (page 129) may work as well for morning routines as they do for summer holiday planning. Once you give something a go, you will soon start to apply the same logic to a variety of situations.

These strategies are for you to pick up alongside your normal parental instincts and practices. They are there to draw upon when you need that bit extra to meet your child's needs.

Using visuals

In many cases, visuals are the simplest and most impactful single thing you can use to support communication and understanding in children. Using visuals might not immediately seem natural to you. But consider it if your child struggles with processing what's going on in their day or what someone is trying to tell them. They might appear lost in a situation, be working to their own agenda or not respond to questions.

Visuals work by making information quicker and easier to process. They can be used instead of words, but more often than not, they are used to support either written or spoken language. They usually consist of rudimentary drawings or symbols of whatever it is they represent. Here are some examples of common visuals:

You can create your own visuals, but most people use online software such as www.widgit.com or www.twinkl.co.uk to download ready-made images. You can get started by using free downloads, but it is probably best to pay for a subscription if you think you will use visuals a lot. A monthly subscription costs about the same as a Netflix account. Free trials are available, and you can cancel the subscription if you aren't using it.

You can also use photos of things or places instead of symbols. This might help to distinguish between this or that park, different grandparents or other places you visit, or if your child struggles to recognize what some of the symbols mean. You might also use photos if you need to communicate something very specific, like a picture of their favourite meal.

> Sometimes, visuals need to be specific so as not to be taken literally. It took my son a while to figure out why he didn't get toast every day for breakfast because the symbol we downloaded and used for 'breakfast' was a picture of some toast.
>
> *Stephen*

Classroom   Playground   Fishfingers, chips and peas

It's best to print and laminate the pictures to create little cards. If you're preparing a sequence, you can print and laminate the whole thing together. You have to embrace your inner primary school teacher and get crafting. If you can't get access to a printer or laminator, your child's school might be happy to do it for you. Although they may not be as specific as you need, a quick search for 'visual aids' on Amazon will show you many of the approaches and resources we're outlining below.

There are a multitude of ways visuals can be used. They can be used on their own, simply as prompts or to reinforce something you're saying. For example, you might hold up a picture of a park and say, 'We're going to the park,' or you might use a picture of a bath to prompt your child when you tell them it's bath time. If you ever go to playgroups or the like, you might see teachers holding cards to prompt children to tidy up or when it's time to sit down in a circle. Often they are used with all children, when there are no particular communication obstacles, simply to reinforce language. There are slightly more involved ways of using visuals too, but none are particularly taxing. Some of the most common techniques are explained below.

Choice boards

A choice board is a visual list of choices you want to give your child. So instead of just saying, 'Shall we go to the park or your nan's house?', you provide pictures of each choice for your child to point at or take off the board. You can use anything as a board, even a scrap piece of cardboard. Velcro strips work well to quickly put choices together on the hoof.

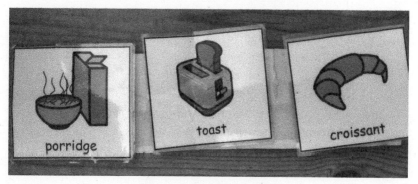

Picture of a choice board

TRANSFORMING OUR CHILD'S MORNING THROUGH USING SIMPLE VISUALS

Stephen describes how visuals helped his son to overcome basic communication barriers and alleviate frustration all round.

When our son was three years old, he had no spoken language and really struggled to communicate. He couldn't yet point, or nod or shake his head, to tell us what he needed. We knew he had a real desire to communicate because he got really frustrated when we didn't know what he wanted; he just needed help to develop some communication skills.

Every morning, he would grunt and scream for what he wanted to eat, and we ran around the kitchen lifting him up and offering anything we could think of to try to find out what was on his mind. It was almost as hard for us as it must have been for him.

Introducing visual supports

By chance, I knew a speech therapist through work, and we invited her over to see if she could help. She observed him for a while, identifying the fact that he had a real desire to communicate but no way to do so. She introduced us to the idea of using visuals. At first, we were a bit hesitant, wondering whether they might even discourage him from learning words, but she reassured us that research evidence said the opposite was true.

The very first thing we did was to create a choice board so our son could choose what he wanted for breakfast. Every day, he could choose bagel, toast or porridge (later we added fruit choices, etc.). For the first time in as long as we could remember, he didn't scream once; and the process took a second, whereas previously it often took several minutes and was really stressful.

Looking back, it seemed such a simple solution, but you don't know what you don't know. The difference was amazing. It was low-tech, impactful and easy to adopt. A win-win!

Now-and-next boards

A now-and-next board does what it says on the tin. It consists of two pictures and the words 'now' and 'next'. The 'now' part is the activity taking place or about to take place. The 'next' part is what will follow. They work well for two reasons: they help to ease anxiety about what's going on and what is expected, and they also help to motivate children through the 'now' if what is 'next' is something to look forward to.

Let's say your child doesn't like taking a shower. If they can play with an iPad after their shower, they may be more inclined to just get the shower out of the way without a fuss in order to get to the activity they want.

This is what a now-and-next board looks like:

The now-and-next board can be used before your child is ready for a whole-day visual timetable (see below) or in addition to a visual timetable. A visual timetable is something that stays the same all day and can be referred back to. A now-and-next board can be whipped out and adapted at opportune moments when it is needed.

For a child who struggles to meet external demands, a now-and-next board might need to be adapted in order to be useful. That might mean your child having a range of options (all agreeable to you and implementable in reality!) of what their 'next' (i.e., their reward) is so that they feel they have some control and an element of choice.

Visual timetables

Visual timetables are a common sight in classrooms. Having one is universally beneficial, whether or not the audience has any SEN. They help children to see quickly what's on throughout the course of a lesson or a day. They help to centre the child and the class in their routine and to reduce uncertainty. If your child is anxious, struggles to regulate their emotions or behaves unpredictably, establishing good routines – backed up by a visual timetable – is one of the best things you can do to help (see page 183 for more information about routines). They also work as effective markers in transitioning between activities, which can help children who find this difficult. They can help to motivate children to complete undesirable tasks to get to the activity they want, much like now-and-next boards (see page 128). They can also help you to limit things you don't want too much of – such as computer gaming – by setting aside a particular time for it.

GETTING STARTED WITH VISUAL TIMETABLES

At first, visual timetables can look complicated: they needn't be. If you've already got your head around using visual prompts, you're halfway there.

The main thing to think about when preparing a visual timetable is the extent to which you break up the day into pieces. Some timetables have only two entries: one for what's happening in the morning and one for what's happening in the afternoon. If your child is already familiar and comfortable with the morning routine of getting dressed, eating breakfast, brushing their teeth, etc., then you don't necessarily need to include all of these things in their timetable. But to see that it's football in the morning and Granny's house in the afternoon can nevertheless be extremely reassuring.

On the other hand, if your child requires more detail and needs to see each specific task on its own, you will need more parts to your timetable. It is common for children to need more detail when they are younger and less detail as they get older, but this isn't always the case. It is also useful to be able to use more detailed timetables at stressful periods – such as holidays or Christmas – when everything is different and your child is out of their usual routine.

MAKING YOUR OWN VISUAL TIMETABLE

To start a timetable, you first need to prepare all the symbols or pictures you will need. Sit down and think carefully about how much detail you want to include in the visual structure of their day and what activities you will need to have on hand to include in the timetable. At the least, you will probably need mealtimes, school and bedtime. You should have visuals for the places you visit the most and the people you see the most.

Next, identify a suitable place to put the timetable. It needs to be displayed prominently and accessed easily. Velcro strips on the fridge door or kitchen cabinet can work well (with the corresponding Velcro on the visual cards themselves). Put a small box or something similar next to it so your child can post the completed activities through a little slot, as if they were posting a letter. Most kids love that part.

Introduce the timetable without a fuss, but be clear about what it is and what it is for. Your child might not react well at first, but be patient. They should soon get into the habit of referring to it and dispensing with the completed activities.

Here is an example of a fairly detailed timetable:

This is an example of the same day but with less detail:

And this version just has the bare bones:

Children often need less detail as they grow up and get used to the world around them. They also become accustomed to what happens when (e.g., always washing your hands before a meal). Thus, in time, fewer specifics may be needed. This may reverse in stressful or uncertain times like holidays, so don't be surprised if it continually evolves. Likewise, your child might cease to need a daily timetable but still benefit from it at weekends if arrangements vary from week to week.

Think broadly about what a visual timetable might be able to support you and your family with. Having an established timetable system might help with putting in place a toileting routine (see page 163), limiting screen time or taking a trip to the supermarket.

Don't be afraid to experiment with how you organize your timetables. See what works best for your family. But do try to stick to it once it's established.

> I always used to prepare the following day's timetable the night before so my son didn't see me putting it together. This helped to reinforce the idea that it was an objective plan and couldn't just be changed willy-nilly.
>
> *Stephen*

Some children struggle with the pressure of what they perceive as externally set demands (see the 'Pathological demand avoidance' section on page 47). Where this is the case, it might be that seeing a visual timetable with 20 predetermined demands adds to the pressure they feel and makes things harder for them. That doesn't mean the approach needs to be abandoned; it might mean offering an element of choice, building parts of the visual timetable together (where it is realistic that some flexibility is offered) or using a question mark visual so the child knows that this is a time for them to choose freely.

Pre-planning and priming

Preparation can often be key to minimizing stress when going to new places or doing new things. Simply seeing what a place looks like, who the people are and what will take place can be massively reassuring.

Imagine yourself going for an important job interview. You might well recce the route to get to the venue beforehand and look up the interviewers on LinkedIn so you know what to expect and can focus on your interview performance instead of worrying about how to get there and who will be asking you questions. Job interviews are particularly anxiety inducing for most people; any new place with different people may feel like this for children with a variety of SEND.

So before you set off to go somewhere new, show pictures of where you are going and whom you will meet. You can also provide a timeline of what will happen during the visit. Google has made this much simpler because most places now have recent photos readily available online. Some common things to prime your child for include:

- visits to the dentist's or doctor's
- holidays – showing pictures of where you will stay
- family get-togethers
- shoe shopping
- visits to the hairdresser's.

Consider what places or events might need to be on your child's list. Some of these things may be required long term, but many of them will only be needed for a while until the 'unknown' element of them is gone. It may be that you use visuals to prime your child about their school or nursery immediately after a school holiday or at any other time they are out of their regular routine.

Being spontaneous

Using visuals doesn't always mean you have to plan in advance. You will know to what degree your child can handle change and unpredictability. Also, sometimes things don't go to plan and you have to improvise. The car might break down, or you might get to your favourite restaurant to find it closed. In these cases, you can always just draw your own pictures to fill in the gaps. You can keep a couple of blank cards handy, or you could keep a small white board on hand to help you communicate any changes.

Stephen shares his experience of using a daily visual timetable with his son.

My son has now largely transitioned out of having a daily visual timetable at home. But if we are doing anything new – particularly if it involves several steps to a journey or new places – I normally simply grab a piece of paper and sketch out a plan for the day with simple line drawings. It's amazing how well he absorbs the visual information compared to verbal information alone. And the drawings can also be comically bad (see below!), which contributes to the fun of the day.

Step-by-step instructions

Step-by-step instructions work really well for tasks that are relatively complex and have multiple steps. Dressing, washing hands and toileting are good examples. We normally take for granted the multitude of intricate steps – and the order they go in – needed to complete everyday tasks. Any child may benefit from having these broken down into manageable steps while they learn and before completing the task becomes second nature. Children who struggle to hold lots of information in mind at the same time find this type of visual guide particularly helpful. This might be because of dyslexia, learning difficulties or autism, for example.

CREATING STEP-BY-STEP INSTRUCTIONS

When you are working on a task or perhaps before you embark on teaching it, think carefully about all the steps you need to follow in order to complete it; think also about the order they go in. This might seem self-evident in some cases, but you would be surprised at how much more complex everyday tasks are when you break them down. Washing your hands, for example, involves a multitude of steps to get the water, soap, rubbing and drying all in the right order, lest you end up with soap on your towel and the tap left on. Look at this example:

Wash hands

135

Everyone needs to wash their hands several times a day. Having this task broken down like this can take the mental strain off a child by simply letting them follow each step in turn. This saves more mental energy for whatever else it is they need to be doing or learning. It can also promote independence and confidence as they may no longer need to be supervised to make sure they have clean hands. This sequence can be laminated and stuck above the sink.

Here is another example – of going to the toilet – which can be located next to the toilet. Notice the last step is washing hands, so all the child needs to do is turn to the sink and there are instructions for that too!

This example also includes photographs of the child's bathroom, which can help a child to connect the abstract to real life.

Using visuals to organize things

A simple way to improve communication is to use symbols as labels around the home. Doing so can improve your child's vocabulary and understanding. It's simple enough: print symbols, accompanied by their names, and stick them with Velcro or tape. You could label kitchen appliances, toy boxes, rooms (on each door) and furniture. The added interest of seeing the cards might spark interactions and conversations, thus aiding communication. Here is an example:

Social stories

Social stories were developed in 1991 by Carol Gray, an American working with autistic children. They were originally intended to target social skills, but the general concepts have since been adapted to suit a much wider variety of needs and are used by parents, carers and professionals for both adults and children with a range of communication differences.

In their most basic form, they are short, explanatory stories written to help somebody understand something. They work by breaking down concepts into bite-size chunks – their constituent parts. This helps children who struggle to take in verbal communication alone and to link concepts and ideas in the way others do (cognition). The stories bridge gaps between what the recipient finds self-evident or already understands (such as where the bathroom is) and related things they don't yet understand (such as why you have to have a bath if you don't want one). Each story has this kind of learning target at its core. They can be as short as a few sentences and as long as is necessary for, and accessible to, the recipient. More often than not, visuals are used in social stories, either to accompany the text or even to replace it altogether. Many ready-made examples can be found online and in books, but try to identify good quality sources. *My Social Stories Book* (Gray, 2002 – see bibliography) is a good place to start.

As well as learning new skills and developing understanding, social stories can also be really effective at preparing children for change – for example, if the child is changing to a new teacher, is extending their nursery school hours to include lunch or is getting into a new weekend routine.

HOW TO WRITE YOUR OWN SOCIAL STORIES

The first step is to identify a learning target. Often this is the easy part. In the example above, the recipient didn't like bathing and didn't understand why it was necessary. The target was to have him learn why it was important and thereby be more willing to bathe regularly.

You will need to judge the level of understanding your child already has and what a realistic learning goal is. Trying to potty train a young child from scratch with a simple story is unlikely to be realistic, but explaining that a child's timetable will start to include visits to the toilet probably would be realistic.

Next, think through the implicit concepts behind the learning point and break them down systematically into simple sentences – something like this:

- We all need to stay clean.
- Philip needs to stay clean.
- To stay clean, we need to wash.
- The bath is for washing yourself.
- Philip can have a bath every day before bed.
- Philip can stay clean by having a bath every day.
- Philip can play in the water!

Adding a fun and positive message at the end of the story is often useful.

Once you have drafted the sentences, add visuals to help get the message across (see page 124). Finished stories can be printed and laminated or even read on an iPad or phone.

Don't be afraid to ask for help when you're trying this for the first time. Often your child's SENDCO or speech therapist would be happy to review and give feedback on stories you write or even help you to write them. It is also good practice for relevant professionals to write social stories for your child to support them in their setting and, if you're lucky, with any challenges you have at home.

Visual timers

For a variety of reasons, some children find changing between activities difficult and even anxiety inducing. This may be because time is an abstract and difficult concept to understand. Or they could find it more difficult to keep in mind the order in which activities are going to take place. As well as using visual timetables, it can also be useful to use a visual timer so your child can see how long is left of the current activity. For example, if there is one hour between coming in from school and dinner time, you could use a one-hour countdown timer to indicate when dinner will start. This may be helpful if your child becomes particularly engrossed in a game or iPad and regularly does not want to stop playing to sit down and eat. Timers can be used for just a few minutes (e.g., to show how long you need to brush your teeth for) or for much longer (e.g., how long you will stay in someone else's house if you need to call on them).

CHOOSING A VISUAL TIMER

There are various types of timer to try. A traditional egg timer or other kitchen timer may work. If your child likes numbers and is able to comprehend them easily, a digital timer might be right for you.

There are also timers designed to be easy to understand visually, which typically display a large colourful disc that retracts behind a plain cover as time passes. These are available in various formats, with the most common looking like a normal, circular clock, in which the circular disc retracts over the course of up to one hour. You set how many minutes you want the timer to last, and the coloured disc retracts in the same way that a minute hand moves towards the top of a clock, getting smaller and smaller until it is fully retracted and no longer visible. Being able to glance at a timer during an activity – or being prompted to do so – can be enough to reassure your child. A search online for '60-minute visual timer' will bring up a range of options that your child might find useful and motivating.

Once your child is used to the timer, the bell or buzzer going off can be enough of a cue for them to move on to the next thing on the timetable without you needing to ask persistently and without your child becoming distressed.

Exceptions to the rule

At the start of this section, we stated that visuals are helpful in many cases. But like all good rules, this one has exceptions. Some children simply do not respond well to them and prefer other ways of communicating. You will recognize how your child responds and adapt accordingly. Some children prefer written communication, for example, or a combination of methods. Use your judgement and proceed with trial and error.

TRUSTING YOUR INSTINCTS – TRIAL AND ERROR

Anil, a young autistic boy, preferred written instructions to the recommended visual cues.

From when he was three years old, we began training Anil to use the toilet following the advice given by professionals. This involved a step-by-step picture guide of using the toilet.

We had no success with this until he was around five-and-a-half, when he started following the pictures but not telling us when he needed to go.

At seven years old, he became better at verbalizing that he needed the toilet. This was because we implemented a whiteboard with visual drawings while also writing several praise words for when he had successfully told us that he needed the toilet and for when he had successfully been to the toilet. The best advice we had was to give him written instructions as opposed to just pictures.

It was combining expert advice with our own knowledge of our child, as well as trial and error, that ultimately helped us to help our son.

Forward- and backward-chaining

Forward-chaining and backward-chaining help with learning sequential tasks; they're particularly good for dressing but have other uses besides.

First, you figure out the sequence. Let's say you are teaching a child to put on shoes with Velcro fastenings. The sequence would go something like this:

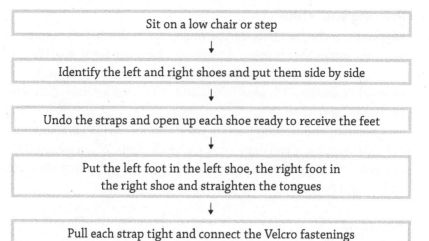

Sit on a low chair or step
↓
Identify the left and right shoes and put them side by side
↓
Undo the straps and open up each shoe ready to receive the feet
↓
Put the left foot in the left shoe, the right foot in the right shoe and straighten the tongues
↓
Pull each strap tight and connect the Velcro fastenings

(Follow with praise and high fives for completing the task)

When using backward-chaining, the child learns the final step in a sequence first. So, in this example, to begin with, the parent would do everything except doing up the straps. Once the child has mastered that step, you teach them the previous one, and so on, until the child can do them all themselves.

Backward-chaining is generally more motivating because the child always has the satisfaction of completing the task themselves by doing the last step.

Forward-chaining works in the opposite way: the child begins by tackling the first step and the parent does the others for them. Once they have mastered the first step, you teach them the second, and so on.

It might be better to use forward-chaining if the first step in a sequence is particularly hard and needs more practice. It can also work better for children who particularly struggle with sequencing itself, because they will learn tasks in their natural order. The downside is they don't get the satisfaction of doing the last step themselves until they have learnt all the others.

Visual prompts and illustrations are particularly useful for learning sequences (see page 124).

Praising your child

We want our children to have a strong sense of self-belief, in spite of learning sometimes being a significant challenge for them. We can find ourselves using 'comfort-focused' feedback – 'Not everyone can be good at maths,' 'It's okay,' 'You and your brother have different strengths,' and so on.

Research conducted by Rattan, Good and Dweck (2012) found this to be disheartening and demotivating for children. When we say, 'Not everyone can be good at maths,' we are implicitly saying that the child will not get better at maths, so why should they try?

And so...?

These researchers found that students perform better and are more motivated about learning if they receive 'strategy-focused' feedback, such as:

- 'You can do better next time if you...'
- 'You only got this one wrong because you...'
- 'Next time, you might try...'

For parents, this means trying to focus (supportively) on how your child can improve at something rather than unintentionally giving them the impression that they cannot improve at something.

Similarly, when our child does succeed, research suggests that we should avoid the temptation to praise their fixed positive qualities ('You're a natural artist,' 'You've always found maths easy'). Instead, Gunderson *et al.* (2013) found that growth mindsets are fostered through praising the processes involved in these successes ('You did well on this because you...', 'If you keep trying hard, you might one day...', etc.).

Building resilience in your child

We all want our children to be a bit more resilient than they are. Or at least, we all hope that they will become more resilient in the future than they are now. For many children, it will feel like this just happens naturally over the course of time.

Researchers (Holdsworth, Turner and Scott-Young, 2018) looked to define what resilient children and young people do (i.e., what helps them to be resilient). They found that resilient children and young people tend to:

- be reflective and keep a sense of perspective
- stay healthy and celebrate successes
- be sociable.

It's easy to see how parents might support this process. Many of the things you do with your child will be achieving this anyway – helping them to reflect on past events, helping them to reflect on the size of a problem, emphasizing the positive and attempting to build their peer network.

While their research focused on the school (rather than the home) environment, there may again be a message here for parents. These researchers found that schools can promote resilience by:

- showing that the classroom is a safe place to experience failure
- showing that failure is a part of learning
- giving feedback that focuses on strategies for succeeding next time.

And so...?

It is not about keeping our children away from failure. Our children need to experience the right balance of challenge and support in order to build their resilience. For parents, it means exposing our children to new experiences that test them at an appropriate level. Endless failure knocks the resilience out of any of us; a lack of challenge stops us from moving forward.

A similar study (Fletcher and Sarkar, 2016) found that resilience is built through creating a 'challenge mindset'. This is potentially really important for parent–child interactions. When our children find something difficult, we should show them that we value the 'hard stuff' to show them that finding something hard leads to learning and development. If our child's 'go-to' reaction when they approach challenge is to give up or tantrum, we might try saying the following things:

WHAT SHOULD I SAY... WHEN MY CHILD IS STRUGGLING WITH A NEW SKILL?

- Show them your own failings, making it clear that we also get things wrong as adults: 'Look at me try to do this... oh dear, Daddy got it wrong AGAIN.'
- Show them *how* they can get better at something (i.e., the strategy they can use), so the problem/challenge no longer feels insurmountable: 'Try looking at the football while you kick it,' 'Slow down your writing and put your hand a little further down the pencil.'
- Break down the challenge/problem so they can experience success in *some* of the task, even if they can't yet master all of it: 'It is hard to cut all those shapes neatly – let's just start with the squares and triangles.'
- Show excitement when something is difficult (a challenge mindset) – remind them when they are failing, more than ever, that you are proud of them, proud of their efforts and proud of the successes they will achieve when they keep going: 'Look how hard you're trying – that's when I see how resilient you can be.'
- Remind them of the progress they have already made: 'I know you're finding the monkey bars hard, but last year you couldn't manage the climbing frame – and look at you now!'

Motivating your child

Sometimes, we *need* our child to do something – brush their teeth, go to school, etc.

Sometimes, we *want* our child to do something – give their auntie a hug, try a new type of food, complete their homework, etc.

In reality, it may feel like life is one long attempt to motivate (or persuade, or coerce) your child to do something that you want/need them to do. Motivating your child to do something they don't want to do can be hard; your knowledge of your child and their response to incentives may be your most valuable tool here.

Where you feel like you've tried everything, it is sometimes worth reflecting on the root cause of their lack of motivation:

- Do they feel unprepared for this next thing?
- Do they have an underlying anxiety about the thing you are asking them to do?
- Do they much prefer the thing they're already doing and not have a clear sense of when they'll be able to do it again?
- Do they understand why the thing they now need to do is important?
- Do they feel pressure associated with meeting an external demand?

Research conducted in educational settings (Jang, 2008) found that student motivation for a task can be enhanced by taking the following steps:

1. Telling students why a task will help them. *Moving from, 'Because I say so(!)' to parents giving a clear sense of why this is important for the child.*
2. Acknowledging students' autonomy in the level of effort they put in, perhaps by giving an element of choice within the task. *'Are you doing your homework in the kitchen or the sitting room?' 'Shall we brush your teeth with your new toothbrush or your old toothbrush?'*
3. Showing students that success is possible for them. *'I was so impressed when you did this yesterday all by yourself.' 'First we do X, then we do Y.'*
4. Acknowledging that the task will be challenging and that struggle is an essential part of the process of learning, not a sign of weakness. *'Sometimes I find it really hard also; finding things hard is really normal.'*

Helping your child to stay in one chair

While there may be many reasons why a child finds it hard to stay in one chair while they complete a task (distractibility, anxiety, sensory needs, motivation for the task, demand avoidance), the reality is that we sometimes need our child to do just this – to eat a meal, to complete their homework, to wait until a parent can help with something, etc.

As a parent, you'll be desperately trying to identify *why* they won't stay in their chair. Be open to the idea that they can't – rather than won't – stay in their chair without some adjustment being made (to the length of time, to the support they have while they're sitting there or even to the chair itself). In addition, see if any of the following might be helpful:

Shorten the task

Consider shortening the length of time you're asking your child to stay in one place for and then build this up over time. Using a timer can support a child to build up their resilience within a task; giving a clear and immediate reward can be a good motivator while this resilience is being built up.

Appreciate the sensory need

Consider sensory supports that might lengthen the amount of time a child can stay in one place. It could be that a wobble cushion is useful. This rubber cushion, filled with air, has a surface that moves while the child sits on it (especially if the child wriggles a lot!). This movement in the cushion can support a child to stay more alert and focused, potentially sitting still for longer because the need to move is taken care of by the movement of the cushion. Alternatively, a 'Theraband' strapped to the legs of a chair can provide a sensory outlet. This means that the child who has an impulse to move or to push can get what they need, while you as their parent get what you're looking for (e.g., your child sits at the table during dinner).

Praise the positive

Go out of your way to notice when things are going well. And when they're not, try non-verbal reminders so that the child – especially a child who pushes back against demands – sees you not as correcting or sanctioning them but as merely reminding them.

Distraction

It may be that engaging your child in a discussion about yester-day's birthday party, singing their favourite song together or doing something else suited to their age, ability or interests is all that is needed.

Build in movement breaks

It may sound counterintuitive to keep your child in one place by allowing them to move, but it could be that a quick movement break ('Run to the kitchen and get a spoon for me,' 'Go to your bedroom to see if the window's open') extends your child's ability to then come back and stay seated.

Reduce the anxiety

If your child leaves their seat because they are anxious (about doing their homework poorly, about the discussion around the dinner table), consider steps to reduce this anxiety. You might use a visual timer that shows them how long they have to remain seated; you might have a visual timetable that shows them what is coming after the current task (be it homework or a mealtime); you might consider a sensory tool such as ear defenders.

Remove your own expectation that they stay in the chair!

Sometimes, the kindest thing to do to yourself and for your child is to know that your current demand is not working for either of you. Although consistent expectations are important, and following through is also important, we can't always 'win'. And as a parent, it's okay to know both that you won't always 'win' and that 'winning' is usually the wrong way to think about parenting a neurodivergent child in the first place. Sometimes, a child's needs mean that our expectations won't be met in quite the way we thought they might. Sometimes, you've just got to know when your child is communicating a need and when/how to try again another time.

Developing writing

For a wide range of reasons, many children struggle with writing. If your child is struggling with writing at any age or stage of their education, their school should be providing you with information about how they are developing your child's writing, potentially with your support at home. The school should know – or be trying hard to find out – whether the issue is about fine motor skills, motivation, understanding or something else entirely.

Clearly, the cause determines the next step, so consider the list below in the context of what your child finds difficult in order to determine a potential way forward:

Developing fine motor skills

Some children struggle to make the right shape with their hand and to sustain it for long enough to write something down. Activities that require careful manipulation of a child's fingers can support the child to eventually control a pencil and formulate letters on a page. Cutting and sticking, play dough or threading can be helpful building blocks of the child's written communication.

Promoting mark-making

Mark-making is a key step towards eventually writing with meaning (i.e., writing letters and words). What may look like a scribble to an adult might be a milestone on the way, at whatever pace, to early literacy. Know, therefore, that mark-making is an important step, even if it appears to be no more than a scribble. What motivates a child to mark-make will be different for different children – it could be felt-tip pens across some sugar paper; it could be fingers in the sand.

Using a programme to support early writing

There are various programmes out there, such as Write From The Start, that build up the level of difficulty from tracing over dotted lines to beginning to form shapes and letters. Your child may find the programme engaging and exciting, especially if you, or a teacher/TA, are there to watch their development and successes. If your child is not motivated to write, however, there is a chance that engagement in such a programme at home may depend on you implementing significant short-term reward.

Making a referral to an occupational therapy service

The method of referring to an occupational therapy (OT) service may depend on where you live, your child's age and whether or not your child has an EHCP. Details of how to refer should be on your local authority's Local Offer website. Alternatively, your child's school

SENDCO or GP can inform you about the way to get your child an OT assessment. See also page 201.

Buying resources that strengthen muscles in the hand

You might buy some 'Theraputty', for example, which, although your child may see it and think of play dough, has the added benefit of giving more resistance than play dough, thereby strengthening muscles in the hand and developing fine motor skills.

Purchasing resources that develop the fine motor control required for writing

'Pencil grips' particularly support children who struggle to hold a pencil or struggle to maintain that hold over a period of time. Writing with a pencil grip can support many children to shape their fingers in a way that will increase their control over the pencil. Pencil grips slot over a pencil and can remove the barrier to writing that your child may be experiencing.

Giving your child help to plan a piece of writing before committing it to paper

Your child might have excellent ideas or know the exact answer to a question but struggle to know how to communicate their ideas on paper. If your child is hesitant to complete written tasks at home, it may help to do some planning together, giving them some notes to help them to get started.

Providing alternative forms of communication, such as speech-to-text software

Most people recognize that handwriting is still an important skill for a child to develop, as long as they have the physical ability to do so. Sometimes, however, it becomes the block that prevents the child from expressing themselves and their thoughts. In this case, allowing the child to dictate their work to a device can be helpful. Common methods of doing this include:

- pressing the mic icon on an iPhone or iPad
- pressing the mic icon on Microsoft Word 365
- clicking 'Voice typing' in the 'Tools' tab on a Google Doc.

Giving your child time

Many dyslexic children, and plenty of children with no diagnosis at all, can write fantastically well if given more time. Understanding that your child writes slowly may be the first step to helping to meet their needs.

Recalibrating what success looks like

Though their sibling may be writing essays, success for a child who finds writing difficult – for any or all of the reasons outlined above – may mean recalibrating how much or how well they can communicate through writing. Praising a well-formed letter, word or sentence (and building up from there) may be exactly what is needed.

Although specialist assessment (i.e., from an OT) is often useful, it is also possible to try some of the things listed above, gauging as you go whether or not they are supporting the development of writing. The view of your child's SENDCO may also be useful here in helping understand what the block to writing might be so that you can both respond accordingly.

Developing reading

There is strong evidence of the impact of parents reading at home with their children (Whitehurst and Lonigan,1998; McConnell and Kubina, 2016), with some studies suggesting that the reading parents do with their children is more important than the reading that happens at school, whether with school staff or through a specialist.

A QUICK WORD ABOUT PHONICS

It is worth pausing for a moment to consider phonics. When the authors of this book were in school, phonics was not the predominant way of learning to read. The focus was the 'whole-word method', in which children would learn to recognize and read key words, building up both their vocabulary and their reading ability in this manner.

Now, the moment your child starts primary school (or perhaps before), you will experience the world of phonics, in which they will learn to read by learning the parts of words. Here are a few things to bear in mind:

There are many different phonics schemes. They have slightly different ways (rhymes, pictures, etc.) of essentially learning the same key sounds in the English language.

The word for a 'sound' in English is a 'phoneme'. Pupils will learn different phonemes during a phonics scheme, starting with the most common/easiest for pupils to learn. They will learn, for example, that the 'ee' sound can be written as 'ee' but can also be written using 'ea' or 'y' (and occasionally with just a single 'e'), depending on the word.

The letter(s) used to write a phoneme is called a 'grapheme'. A phonics scheme will take the common graphemes and teach them to pupils in groups, usually with a rhyme and/or picture to help them to 'stick'. They will learn, for example, that the 'k' sound can be written using a 'k' or 'ck'.

To people of a certain age, the synthetic phonics approach makes the alphabet feel a bit redundant. The alphabet becomes a nice song to sing in class, but what pupils are actually learning is the sounds (phonemes) that those letters make. And they don't even learn them in alphabetical order!

Whereas no parent should be expected to become a reading expert merely because their child has SEND, it may be important to know the fundamentals in order to support them at home.

Diagnosing a reading issue

THE LIMITATIONS OF A 'READING AGE'

As children get older, the school may report to parents their child's 'reading age' – they may tell you that your 12-year-old has 'a reading age of seven years four months', for example.

It's worth exercising a bit of caution when viewing this number. Its limitation lies in the following facts:

- It only describes how someone does on that day, with that test.

- It doesn't capture the complexity of what being good at reading involves (being able to decode a word, having a wide vocabulary, being able to take meaning from a text, etc.).
- It doesn't capture a child's underlying motivation to read.

If your child's school report a reading age that sounds a bit lower than you think is correct, you might choose to ask:

- what in particular the child struggles with in regard to reading
- what the school plan to do to support the child's reading development (and, possibly, what could be done at home to support them).

UNDERSTANDING THE BARRIER

Improving a child's reading can only really happen once you know what the barrier is to their reading development. A conversation with the school, as well as your own observations, should help you to see if it is any of the following:

- **Pre-phonics**: For some children, their neurodivergence means they may not be developmentally ready to formally learn to read, even when other children their age are. Trying to force phonics on a child who is not there yet developmentally can be at best a waste of everyone's time and at worst a thing that turns the child off reading longer term.
- **Phonics**: Your child may not have a secure knowledge of the common phonemes (sounds) and the graphemes (letter or combination of letters) that represent them on the page.
- **Fluency**: Your child may be able to read but not at speed or in a way that has a natural flow (or fluency) to it.
- **Comprehension**: Your child may be able to read accurately but may struggle to take meaning from what they read.

The list of potential barriers is almost endless. You could add to this list eyesight (a child has the ability to read but is long-sighted), motivation (a child could read wonderfully if only they were motivated to do so), dyslexic difficulties around readability, etc. A first step for a parent might be to learn what the barriers are from the nursery/school so they know how they might support them at home and with what.

STARTING TO READ WITH AN ALTERNATIVE APPROACH TO PHONICS
Stephen describes a tailored approach for his son.

Our son has a speech sound disorder, meaning he struggles to pronounce the whole range of sounds we use in English. We don't know whether he can hear them well or not. He is aware of this on some level and is regularly apprehensive about speaking aloud when asked to, answering questions, etc.

The regular phonics approach of learning to reproduce sounds and putting them together to decode words did not work for him. If anything, it disengaged him in his learning. Luckily, his (special) school decided to use a more nuanced approach and adopted a 'word recognition' programme for him. Using this method, he quickly learnt common words and was able to start to recognize and say them aloud, i.e., to read. It was individualized, nuanced, and played to his strengths. They even used vocabulary from subjects he was interested in to get him more on board.

Phonics is supposed to be mandatory in schools in England, but we agreed with our son's teacher that we wouldn't tell the government if she didn't! This whole process was a reminder that the evidence might tell you what works for many pupils, but things always need to be considered in the context of an individual child, especially when that child has SEND.

Understanding an appropriate response
Once you know what the issue is, an appropriate response might be as follows:

PRE-READING
For some children, their cognition or language development will mean that trying to get them to sit down and recognize graphemes is not a good use of anyone's time.

Just because a child is not yet ready for phonics doesn't mean you should abandon your commitment to helping them to one day become a fluent reader; you just prioritize slightly different things. Rather than teaching the link between the sounds (or phonemes) and the letters that form them (or graphemes), you might first lay the foundations for reading by doing the following things:

- **Prioritizing exposure to language**: Developing your child's language is different to teaching your child to read, but it can be a transformative step in that direction. Language might be developed through simple word games ('I spy', 'I'm thinking of a person...', categories, etc.) in addition to any language programme being implemented by your child's school, nursery or SALT.

  The more language-rich your child's environment, the more you are supporting their vocabulary development – vital for any successful reader. That is likely to mean maximizing the quantity and quality of spoken interactions with your child. The ShREC approach from the Education Endowment Foundation (EEF) provides an evidence-informed framework for such high-quality interactions, containing four key elements: shared attention between you and the child; responding to what the child is telling you; expanding on what they're telling you; and extending the interaction so it resembles a conversation (albeit appropriate to the child's age and ability, often including non-verbal communication). The EEF (n.d.) has a useful graphic explaining what evidence-informed adult–child interactions might look like.

- **Promoting an enjoyment of learning**: Though your child may not be sitting and reading to you yet, show them that learning – particularly around language – can be fun. This might be through songs that you sing together, word games you play together or nursery rhymes you recite together.

- **Promoting a love of reading**: Your own interest in their books is likely to be a highly motivating factor (see the 'Motivation' section below). The chance to put on your best voices and be the characters in their favourite story promotes this passion for storybooks. Such a passion for stories will often support a child to give written text their full attention, which will be vital when it comes to phonic development.

PHONICS

If your child doesn't have a secure understanding of phonics, be sure to use the same approach as the programme used at the school/nursery. The multitude of different phonics programmes out there achieve largely the same thing, but the rhymes/images they use to get there are often quite different. Consistency with school will be key here.

FLUENCY

A common approach to developing fluency is echo reading, in which (as the name suggests) the parent reads a line of text, and the child follows by reading the same line of text. This way, the child gets a better sense of the prosody (intonation, stress, rhythm) of the text, developing their ability to read fluently. It is generally recommended that the parent reads a whole book aloud to the child first, before going back to read it again with an echo-reading approach.

COMPREHENSION

Your child might read with a high level of accuracy but seem to have very little understanding when you talk to them about the content. The phonics and fluency are there, but reading comprehension is the block. There is evidence (Education Endowment Foundation, 2019) behind four 'reciprocal reading' strategies that adults can adopt to promote and monitor comprehension when hearing their children read. When listening to your child read, try the following four approaches:

- **Predicting**: Look at the title, the front cover or a chapter's title. Engage your child's interest in the book by asking them to make a prediction.
- **Questioning**: At the end of a sentence, page or chapter, ask your child a question about what they (or you) have just read. If your child doesn't know the answer, reread the same section, make your question easier or focus on the tricky word/phrase that might prevent meaning being taken.
- **Clarifying**: If a word hasn't been understood, teach its meaning. You might tell your child its definition but also use it in a sentence and ask your child to use it in a sentence; you might then ask them to use it again a few minutes later (or if this is too challenging, use it yourself again in a few minutes). This

repetition at intervals will often support retention of new vocabulary.

- **Summarizing**: At the end of a paragraph, page or chapter, ask your child to summarize what they have just read. This is a challenging skill for many children, but it will give you a sense of the comprehension level of your child.

MOTIVATION

Some children, for a multitude of reasons, just aren't motivated to read. For parents, there is a tricky balance (as with all things) in deciding when to push ('let's have a go at this word again') and when pushing would be the most demoralizing and demotivating thing possible. There are any number of things a parent can do to try and increase a child's motivation for reading:

- **Ensure the child experiences success**: Perhaps by asking them to read just one or two words per page, for example, while you read the rest.
- **Find books of interest**: It can be hard to find books for readers who aren't reading at the same level as their peers. Few ten-year-olds still want to be reading about Biff and Chip. For books that are written for an older chronological age but a younger reading age, look at the Rapid Plus series of books or books published by Barrington Stoke.
- **Make reading part of a routine**: Although bedtime is favoured for this, there are also disadvantages (the child's tiredness; perhaps some anxiety about getting to sleep, for some children). It may be that looking at a book together with a biscuit straight after school becomes a motivating routine.
- **Reward!** We all find ourselves rewarding our children when there are things they're not inherently interested in doing (getting dressed for school, giving their grandma a cuddle or eating their broccoli).

Studying at home

We know that the education system has exams at the heart of it and that our exam system requires pupils to retain knowledge and to recall or apply that knowledge. We also know that knowledge can be more securely retained when it is revisited regularly, which is why schools typically expect pupils to access some of their learning at home as they get older, via homework or revision tasks.

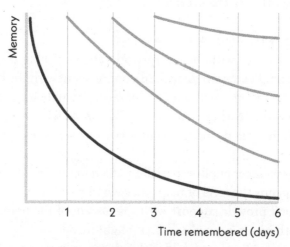

The forgetting curve

This 'forgetting curve', from Ebbinghaus's famous study, shows that frequently revisiting previously visited learning supports it to move into long-term memory.

Helping your child with their homework

It is helpful for our children if we can support them to revisit what they've learned. But what might that look like for a parent when children have a frequent distaste for doing homework?

REWARD SUCCESS

Children respond to incentives, as we know. Consider what reward system would work most successfully for your child in relation to revision and homework (access to a motivating game or toy, time on the tablet, a token system that leads to a bigger reward, etc.).

Also consider what kinds of tasks should be rewarded in relation to homework or revision. Spending 20 minutes in their room with a book open isn't success (and isn't worthwhile) per se; writing a summary of Chapter 1, or doing five maths questions, may well be.

REGULAR BREAKS

Homework can seem very overwhelming for children, especially when they have additional needs. When they know they can take breaks, this anxiety can be lessened; it should also mean your child works more effectively between the breaks.

NOT DOING TOO MUCH AS A PARENT

Helping your child with their homework can be a double-edged sword. Though it might support your child's engagement with the homework and might get them a better mark/comment from their teacher, it also only shows the teacher what your child can do with support rather than what they can do independently. Here are some ways around this:

- For younger pupils especially, put a note on the homework that explains the level of help you gave them with it.
- Don't provide support with the *content* of the homework but with *how it is completed*. That might mean:
  - providing your child with a distraction-free space in which to work (where possible!)
  - goal-setting ('let's aim for three questions in the next 15 minutes, then a quick break')
  - helping them to reflect on how successfully they completed a homework task.

> Parents can support their children by encouraging them to set goals, plan, and manage their time, effort, and emotions. This type of support can help children to regulate their own learning and will often be more valuable than direct help with homework tasks.
>
> *Education Endowment Foundation (2021)*

Helping your child to revise

Children who are a bit older and preparing for exams may well be expected to revise at home. For some children with SEND, revising effectively can be a real challenge.

LITTLE AND OFTEN

Teachers will often talk about 'spacing' as an effective way to support pupils to learn. Spacing is the opposite of cramming. Finding frequent opportunities to revisit content over a period of time is more likely to support learning than your child cramming at the last moment. Spending 15 minutes each day on structured revision over the course of a week is likely to bring better results than 90 minutes of revision the night before the exam.

QUIZZING

Ebbinghaus's 'forgetting curve' (above) shows us what can happen when pupils are 'quizzed'. The term 'quizzing' is often used in education when we don't want to put pupils off by calling it 'testing'. 'Testing' feels high-stakes; 'quizzing' is about the process of trying to remember something for the purpose of learning rather than for the purpose of passing/failing a test.

Research suggests that, for a child, the process of being asked to try and remember something is more useful for learning than simply being told something again. With your child, that might mean asking them a few questions from a textbook, particularly in the run-up to exams. Crucially, it means not giving them the answer too quickly but waiting while they try to remember it.

NOT JUST READING, COPYING OR HIGHLIGHTING

Many children don't know how to revise. Yet there are schools that still give pupils the instruction 'to revise' without giving a specific task and without teaching the skills needed to revise.

The important thing for parents to understand is that merely reading something is not a particularly effective revision technique; it is far more impactful if pupils are actively completing a task that involves a thought process – typically not just copying or randomly highlighting.

Ideally, the school sets pupils a task that helps them to revise effectively. Failing this, you might need to work with your child on such a task, for example, rewriting a passage from a textbook in their own words, summarizing the key points from a page of notes or coming up with relevant questions that they can then answer.

CHAPTER 4

LIFE AT HOME

In this chapter, we look a bit further than formal learning, towards things that are no less vital in the life of a family. We consider how to address your child not sleeping, how to support them to gain more independence in their morning routines and how to go about managing sibling relationships.

We hear from many parents, who outline the ways they achieve success in their home and family life, with an appreciation that success means different things to different families and with an acknowledgement that success often feels out of reach for many parents of children with SEND. We hear from those who are parenting differently to how they themselves were parented and learn about their experiences of parenting 'outside the norm'. We hear about their successes, which they have often achieved by accepting that children with differences sometimes require parents to think a bit differently too.

Sleep

Sleep is a chemically driven process that is universal across all animals. Sleeping well is important for health and for the good of the family.

Unfortunately, for a variety of reasons, problems with sleep are more common in children with SEN. It could be because a child finds it difficult to relax or because of anxiety. It could also be due to a difference in the sleep hormone melatonin or a medical condition such as epilepsy. Poor sleep has been linked to hyperactivity, greater difficulties in learning, low mood and even obesity.

As any parent of a newborn baby can attest, a sustained lack of sleep can also be incredibly difficult to manage for the whole household. It is therefore important that sleep issues are identified and alleviated where possible.

Sleep hygiene

Children between three and five years old should sleep for 10–13 hours on average (including naps). Children aged six to twelve need 9–12 hours on average (Great Ormond Street Hospital, 2023). If your child is finding it difficult to get to sleep, not sleeping enough, wakes frequently or has another sleep-related problem, the first thing to do is evaluate your child's 'sleep hygiene'.

Good sleep hygiene is not about one single intervention or solution to a sleep problem. Rather, it is a general view of the sleep environment and sleep-associated behaviour. You can use the following checklist to identify how you might provide your child with the best chance of a good night's sleep:

- ☐ Use blinds/curtains to eliminate natural light during sleep hours (especially in summer when sunset is late in the evening).
- ☐ If there is any light in the bedroom, it should be soft, red in colour and not bright enough to be able to read. Avoid blue light in the bedroom.
- ☐ The bedroom should not be too hot or too cold.
- ☐ The bed itself should only be used for sleeping: no eating or watching TV in bed.
- ☐ Avoid caffeine.
- ☐ Children should be outdoors to absorb daylight for at least 30 minutes every day.
- ☐ Avoid vigorous exercise before bedtime.
- ☐ Avoid iPads, etc. for at least an hour before bed.
- ☐ Keep the bedroom quiet.
- ☐ Follow a set bedtime routine (e.g., bath time, bedtime story, etc.).
- ☐ Go to bed and get up at the same time each day.
- ☐ Avoid large quantities of food and drink before bed. The exception to this is a glass of warm milk because it can help the body produce and release melatonin.

☐ Younger children should avoid naps later in the afternoon.

Adapted from Children and Family Health Devon (n.d.)

What to do about issues with sleep

If your child has sleep issues, you can try keeping a sleep diary to identify particular triggers or patterns. Note down what your child eats, what time they sleep and wake up, and anything else that's relevant. Review this after a few weeks to see if there is a particular stimulus affecting your child or if you could improve their sleep hygiene. You can also strengthen some of the elements of good sleep hygiene with additional strategies designed for children with communication or sensory differences. For example, visual cues and social stories (see page 137) can help to establish your routines. Wind-down activities (such as guided breathing or massage) may also help as part of your routine.

Further support
Go to your health visitor or GP
Occupational therapy (see page 201)
Talk to your child's SENDCO
Scope www.scope.org.uk/advice-and-support/ help-disabled-child-sleep
The Sleep Charity https://thesleepcharity.org.uk
Contact https://contact.org.uk/help-for-families/information- advice-services/health-medical-information/ common-concerns/helping-you-and-your-child-sleep

If you are already following guidance on good sleep hygiene and your child is still experiencing problems with sleep, various other things may help. You may be supported to try behavioural approaches designed to help your child into a better routine. These include, for example, the gentle withdrawal of your presence from your child's bedside to encourage them to sleep independently. There are also medical interventions such as supplementary melatonin, but these must be recommended by a specialist. You can talk to your GP about your child's sleep, who may refer you to a specialist clinic. Your local authority or NHS trust may also offer support. Your child's school may be able to help you access the help you need.

Toileting and self-care

Toileting is a universal human need and is one of the most important skills for a child to learn. It has an impact on social and family life and benefits self-esteem, relationships and future participation in life and education. For these reasons, it is important that every child is supported to achieve their full potential in toileting. This may not always mean full, independent continence, however.

Most children become physically able to control bladder and bowel functions between the ages of two and three. Although bowel and bladder maturity typically develops at the same time for everybody, cognitive capacity and differences, communication limitations, motivation, demand avoidance, motor development and sensory differences may contribute to difficulties in toileting for children with special needs.

Not all children with special needs will learn later than average. Likewise, many children without special needs have difficulties in toilet training or learn later than average. That said, learning difficulties can and do commonly affect both *when* and *how* children with SEND learn to transition from nappies to independent continence.

Toilet learning

Helping your child to learn can feel like an insurmountable undertaking, especially if they need to learn in a completely different way to most children. It's important you feel mentally and practically prepared to begin. If you don't know where to start, don't worry; there is help out there. Your job is to identify a pathway that's right for your child and to keep going through any pitfalls, adapting your approach and celebrating successes as you go.

Assuming that your child does need additional support and you need to understand more yourself, start by doing some research into toileting in general and into your child's condition in relation to toileting (we've started you off with some links in 'Further support' at the end of this section). It is easy to underestimate the complexity of going to the toilet and quite how much we expect of very young children. As well as recognizing the need to go, there is clothing to contend with, the sensory environment of a bathroom and a particular order in which everything must be done. Part of the key to making progress with toileting is understanding your child in relation to all the different elements they need to master.

Toileting plans

After doing your research, it's a good idea to write a toileting plan you can share with relatives, your child's school and any therapists (see pages 232–234 for an example of a plan). A plan might include information about your child and their existing habits, the language they use, aids they require and a step-by-step timeline for making progress with toileting. Refer to the resources below for more information about how to make plans for your child.

Using visuals

It is common practice to use visual supports and social stories to support children's understanding. Visual supports and sequences can be stuck with Blu-Tack next to the toilet. Social stories can be used both to describe the process of using a toilet and to explain changes or progress you want your child to make (e.g., to use public toilets instead of a potty when out and about).

Read more about using visuals in the section on page 124, which includes an example of step-by-step instructions for using the toilet.

Additional support

Many specialist support materials exist that go into more detail than the scope of this section. ERIC – The Children's Bowel and Bladder Charity – is the UK's leading charity in the field. Its website hosts a wealth of information and resources and it even runs a helpline at certain times during the week. Bladder & Bowel UK supports adults and also has information about children. Charities supporting specific special needs, as well as certain professional agencies, can also offer support and advice.

In terms of tangible supports, as well as the usual child toilet seats and steps, your child may benefit from additional items such as handrails. Specialist companies sell adaptive clothing and accessories you may need. Occupational therapists are the experts in this area, but charities and other contacts can also help (see 'Further support' at the end of this section).

TOILET TRAINING OUR AUTISTIC SON
Trusting in professional advice really worked for this family.

When our son was two and before we knew he was autistic, we tried potty training several times, all of which were unsuccessful. We even asked friends for tips and read a few mainstream books on the subject, but we made very little progress.

At age three-and-a-half, our son was showing more and more signs of being able to toilet independently. For example, he would stay dry for longer periods during the day and he would stop what he was doing and notice when he was weeing in his nappy. We were also aware that he was probably the only one his age at nursery still in nappies and we were worried this would affect how he felt.

Tackling this felt like a massive undertaking and I had no clue how to start. He lacked the comprehension and communication needed to learn in a typical way. But I really felt he was ready to learn to use a toilet. I had a goal in the back of my mind that he would be out of nappies by his fourth birthday. That felt like a realistic aim.

Finding some advice
Not knowing where to start, I looked on the website of the National Autistic Society and identified a specialist book on the subject called *Toilet Training and the Autism Spectrum* (Fleming and MacAlister, 2016). I read the book from cover to cover and simply put my faith in the authors' knowledge and followed whatever it recommended. I wrote a toileting plan and started implementing it.

At first, it consisted of really small steps – such as adding toilet time to our visual timetable – and slowly but surely it started to work. The whole process took about six months; it wasn't all plain sailing, but we got there in the end. It was a massive achievement all round. At the time, it felt like the biggest achievement of my life – even more than completing a university degree.

Looking back, I'm really happy I was able to find a way to help my son. Seeing our little boy take himself to the toilet to do a wee for the first time was incredible!

To other parents feeling like they have a mountain to climb, I would say have faith that your child will be able to learn (as far as they are able) with the right support. Figuring out the puzzle for your child can give you a massive sense of achievement, and don't worry about the setbacks along the way – there is no right or wrong path, as every child is different. Whether or not your child is autistic, I would highly recommend the book I used.

Further support

Go to your health visitor or GP	
Occupational therapy (see page 201)	
Talk to your child's SENDCO	
Recommended reading (not just for parents of autistic children)	*Toilet Training and the Autism Spectrum* (Fleming and MacAlister, 2016)
ERIC www.eric.org.uk	
Bladder & Bowel UK www.bbuk.org.uk	

Clothing

For a variety of reasons, many children with SEN benefit from adaptive clothing. It is common for autistic children to be particularly sensitive to itchy fabric or spikey labels and seams. Children with motor planning difficulties such as dyspraxia may find it difficult to tie shoelaces and fasten tight buttons. Children with physical differences, incontinence, feeding tubes and stomas may also need specialist clothing.

Some adaptations are relatively simple and widely available, such as seamless underwear or pull-on shirts. Others are highly specialist and may require more research to find. Normally, charities supporting the particular need of your child will be able to advise on options. Other families can tell you what worked for them.

As well as small, specialist manufacturers and retailers, high street brands have started to produce adaptive clothing to meet market demand and support their customers. These include general clothing, swimwear and school uniforms. Asda and Marks and Spencer have 'easy dressing' school uniform ranges; the latter having worked with the National Autistic Society to develop and trial its products.

Your child's school may be able to help and advise. Schools should be able to relax uniform policies to ensure they are inclusive – some parents find this an easy discussion to have with their child's school, while others face some opposition from the school. A mutual agreement can normally be reached, in which the child adheres to as many aspects of the uniform policy as is possible for them while also being comfortable enough to learn efficiently and to have a positive experience of school.

Further support
Talk to your child's SENDCO
Contact charities supporting your child's needs
Search for retailers online

Dressing

Dressing is complicated. It takes time and effort to learn how to put on clothes, to understand the order they go in and to master how to use the various fastening types such as buttons, zips and laces. As such, parents often find it easier and quicker to dress their children rather than have children dress themselves. It's particularly hard to find the time and patience to help children learn when everyone is rushing around in the morning trying to get to school and work on time.

Most families simply bumble along, and at some point, the child picks up enough to make themselves more or less presentable for school. But this process can take much longer if your child has additional needs and finds it harder to learn. And as parents, we often find it easier to keep doing things for them for longer. Luckily, there are some simple strategies you can use to help, and one of the easiest is forward- or backward-chaining (see page 140). You can use this technique to help your child learn other things once you understand the principle. Step-by-step visual instructions are also really useful (page 124).

Helping your child to help themselves

Boring as it may be for some people, being organized in and around the home can go a long way towards helping your child be more independent. If they struggle with completing complex tasks (sometimes called 'executive functioning') or can't see or do things as quickly as others, being well organized can really help them along the way.

It can be really stressful and even impossible to get things done if they aren't consistently organized. Try to avoid a house in which clean school uniforms could be in any one of three places, shoes may or may not be on the rack in the porch and you leave at different times every day. Put clothes in the same place ready to put on. Keep the bathroom free at the same time. And if you need to nip to the shop, go once you've dropped your child off rather than rushing everyone to leave ten minutes early; for some children, even small changes like this can really add up and negatively affect the rest of their day (for more information about routine, see page 183).

Eating

Food is emotive for us as parents. We have an in-built desire to provide for our child, and where we can't provide for them, it's very easy to feel like a failure.

Many children with SEND will have a more complicated relationship with food; therefore, their parents may find it harder to provide their child with a healthy, balanced and varied diet.

This might be because the child has physical needs that affect things like the ability to chew or swallow. It might be because the child has allergies and intolerances that restrict the range of foods available to them. It might be because they have sensory differences related to food. Or it might be because a child is demand avoidant and the expectation to eat foods they haven't chosen is something they push against or avoid.

In terms of what to do next, sources of advice will often be child specific – they may require the input of a medical professional who knows your child (whose advice, of course, replaces what we suggest below).

Other sorts of advice may be more widely applicable, although perhaps still provided by a specialist – a nutritionist or dietician, for example, which is typically accessed through your child's GP.

Start with what they will eat

Your child getting enough food is the number-one goal. If they're not, get professional help.

All children need a nutritious diet, and all children deserve exposure to a wide range of foods, but not being hungry is still the number-one goal. It's worth keeping this initial goal in mind if you're particularly preoccupied with how many different fruits and vegetables they're eating.

The culinary goalposts often look different for children with SEND. The most positive relationship you can have with your child around food might mean they eat slowly, little and often, without typically expected table manners, in a different part of the house or with an enormous sense of repetition.

It's not about giving up on your child or accepting that they will always have a highly restrictive diet (though they might); it's just about knowing that the pace of change may look very different. It's about knowing that experiences of eating out may not be the same for your family and that the excitement of a well-prepared Christmas dinner or Eid al-Fitr feast may not be universally felt.

You might therefore recognize that consistency is important and ensure you provide that consistency for your child. That might mean always providing dry Cheerios in the same bowl for breakfast, arriving to school pickup with a particular snack or never changing your brand of peanut butter. These can be as much about the comfort of a familiar routine as they are about the food itself.

You might also recognize opportunities to slowly try to expand your child's diet. You'll do this at times when your child is feeling a bit more resilient, probably choosing foods that are similar to those they already eat – a toasted bagel instead of toast or a different flavour of smoothie than the preferred option (though with both original options on hand just in case!).

It comes down to the point at the start of this section though – not being hungry is the number-one goal.

Offer choice

Choice can be overwhelming for children, but it can also be liberating. Offering choices that are palatable to you as their parent (and their cooker of food!) and that the child can work with can be the way to ensure a win-win outcome. As mentioned in previous sections, choices can be offered visually (see page 124) where a child is easily overwhelmed with language or where a child is unable to consistently use language.

With research evidence suggesting a link between autism and difficulties with managing blood sugar levels (Sala *et al.*, 2020), an approach that prioritizes the child not being hungry may well be needed merely to keep your child healthy. That might sometimes mean abandoning your two pre-prepared choices in favour of your child getting something to eat.

Understand your child's sensory relationship with food

Food can be a very common way for sensory preferences to play out. One child's hypersensitivity might lead them to only eat very plain (and often beige) food. Another child's hyposensitivity might see them always seeking stronger flavours, such as pickled, sour or bitter foods.

Taste is of course only one aspect of a child's sensory relationship with food. They might struggle to tolerate a food smell that others in the family barely notice. They might be particularly bothered by the sound of a family member eating or the feeling of a fork scraping on a plate. They might struggle with mixed textures, requiring food to be separated on a plate, or with the feel of sloppy foods in their mouth.

Your child's sensory profile may be as unique as them. Being alert to and respectful of a child's sensory needs can be a first step to understanding how to make mealtimes (and eating more generally) more successful for you all.

Stay positive

It can be very easy to create anxiety in children around food. When they won't taste the thing *they asked for* or won't try the thing *you've prepared specially*, our own frustrations as a parent can come out.

By appreciating that your child *can't* eat typically – rather than *won't* eat typically – it can be easier to understand their difficulties and to keep eating a positive experience. Trying to *make* them eat a certain diet won't do any good and may cause resentment and further issues.

If your child doesn't eat what you've prepared or isn't growing into the food connoisseur you wish them to be, don't feel like you're failing. As long as you provide a balanced diet and don't give up on your child, that's all you can do. When all is said and done, you cannot ultimately control how they react and what they will and will not eat.

Bilingual and multilingual families

There are various situations in which multilingualism becomes possible. There may be a family with one parent who has English as a first language and one who does not. Both parents may share the same language that is not English, or each parent could have a first language that is not English. Both parents may have English as a first language but belong to a cultural group with its heritage (and perhaps grandparents) who speak another language. Households may include grandparents of other relatives who have other languages and perhaps do not speak English. Indeed, the linguistic nature of families can be as diverse as the make-up of families themselves.

Gone are the days when multilingual families were urged to sideline languages that weren't English. It was thought to confuse and disadvantage children if they didn't focus on English – the language of their forthcoming education and work life. Instead, nowadays, a multilingual cultural heritage is seen as a boon. Being able to communicate in more than one language is more important than ever in today's 'global economy'. Moreover, learning to navigate more than one social and linguistic context can help to develop cultural and emotional awareness and supports flexible thinking.

Children are naturally good learners of languages and are hardwired to pick up on different registers and how children and adults speak differently to each other. For children, other languages are simply another piece of the jigsaw, and they tend to adapt to them easily. They will also pick up on which language is viewed as most important by adults, so if you want your child to value a language, you must convey that.

Some children of multilingual families may make more mistakes for a bit longer when trying to speak only one language, but this does not normally last. The most important things are to be consistent (e.g., stick to one language per parent or one language for the home) and to provide a language-rich environment. There is no reason in particular to change your set-up if your child has SEN, although it is impossible to rule out every eventuality and adaptation you may need to make.

THE GIFT OF BILINGUALISM

Here, Husna shares how she approaches exposing her daughter to her own language as well as to English.

I am the mother of a seven-year-old girl. I am of Moroccan origin, but I grew up in Italy from the age of nine and therefore I speak both Arabic and Italian. My daughter was born in Italy, and we moved to the UK when she was eight months old, so for the first months of her life I spoke to her in Italian and I saw that she interacted with me, but after moving to the UK I had to learn English, so I started mixing the three languages – Italian, Arabic and English.

At the age of two, she started nursery, but she was non-verbal so it was suggested that I speak only one language with her, so I chose English. Until she was three-and-a-half, I was struggling to find the right method to communicate with my daughter, reading articles on the subject, asking experts – but everyone said different things.

At age four, after receiving her EHCP, we managed to find a place in her current school, where the first day the head teacher heard me speaking to her in English, she said to me, 'Why don't you speak to her in your language? She will still learn English here at school, and don't be afraid to mix languages – she will absorb everything like a sponge.'

At the beginning, I thought that my daughter's delay in speaking was my fault because I mixed several languages. Today, I can say that my bilingualism is a gift that will help my daughter to interact with more and more people. Today, she talks about video games with cousins in Italy and tells her day to her grandparents in Morocco, with some help.

Travel and outings
Sunflower lanyards

People wear sunflower lanyards around the neck as a discreet way to indicate to staff or people around them that they may need help or more time because of a non-visible disability. They are especially appropriate for people with auditory or visual differences, neurological conditions such as autism and cognitive impairments such as learning difficulties and dementia, as well as mental health conditions. Some people with physical disabilities also choose to wear them, and they are now a relatively common sight in public.

Since its launch at Gatwick Airport in 2016, the scheme has been officially adopted by all airports and the railway network in the UK and various other agencies and businesses. It is also growing internationally. Although awareness of the scheme is still not universal, it is widespread enough that people are likely to recognize the meaning of the sunflower even if you are not in a location officially signed up to the scheme.

GETTING A SUNFLOWER LANYARD

If you choose to get a sunflower lanyard for your child, you should buy it from the official Hidden Disabilities charity. They are not free, but the price is very modest. You can choose to wear the lanyard on its own or with a badge displaying the disability and/or name and contact information.

It can be handy to keep a lanyard with you just in case you or your child is feeling under pressure in public. Being able to slip it on when you're catching a train, visiting a museum or stopping at a busy service station can be quite reassuring, even if special arrangements aren't necessarily needed. Not feeling like you need to account for your child's differences in the eyes of others can be one less thing to worry about.

Further support

Hidden Disabilities online store
https://hiddendisabilitiesstore.com

THE PARENT'S GUIDE TO SEND

Using accessible public toilets

Accessible toilets are designed to meet the needs of wheelchair users and people with other disabilities, including those with bowel or bladder conditions. Your child with SEN may or may not need to use accessible toilets, depending on the nature of the need. If using an accessible toilet makes toileting easier and less stressful *because of your child's individual needs*, then you should use them. This can be for a multitude of reasons including, for example, an acute sensitivity to noise. The sound of hand dryers can be particularly distressing and lead to a reluctance to use the toilet. Remember, however, that just because public toilets can be crowded and unpleasant to use, this alone is not a reason for using the accessible option!

Different public places have different policies on the use of accessible toilets, so it may be worth familiarizing yourself with these. Fortunately, awareness of 'non-visible' disabilities is increasing, and you shouldn't be made to feel like you need to explain yourself when accessing accessible toilets.

The National Key Scheme (RADAR keys)

Out and about, you may have noticed that many accessible public toilets are locked and require a key. The long-established National Key Scheme (formerly the RADAR Key Scheme) aims to standardize entry to accessible toilets and prevent their misuse. There are now thousands of toilets nationwide to which access is gained by using a RADAR key. Luckily, you don't need to fill in any forms or provide proof of a disability to get a key, you just need to purchase one from the charity Disability Rights UK. The keys cost £6 and are dispatched by post.

Once you have a key, keep it with you when you are out and about; it can really take the stress out of using public toilets. Places like motorway service stations can often be crowded, have queues and be very noisy. Knowing that your child with additional needs can quickly access a toilet when needed can be very reassuring and increase your child's access to everyday spaces and activities. If this is the case, accessible toilets are serving their purpose.

Further support

Disability Rights UK
https://shop.disabilityrightsuk.org/products/radar-key

Blue Badges

The Blue Badge parking scheme has been around for decades and exists to make it easier for people who cannot walk, or who have other disabilities limiting mobility, to park closer to their destination than would otherwise have been possible. Having a Blue Badge can open up otherwise inaccessible public places and activities and can be life-changing for people for whom mobility is an issue.

GETTING A BLUE BADGE

Although the scheme is national, it is administered by local authorities. Applications are made to local authorities and there are some small differences in how the scheme operates in different areas. There is a modest fee for applying for a badge, but this can be offset because parking is often free, whereas you would otherwise need to pay for it. The badge stays with the disabled person – not a particular vehicle – which is useful if your child travels in various cars.

You can check if your child is eligible by reading the guidance from your local authority before making an application. Some people qualify automatically, and others require the local authority to make an assessment of the application, for which they may request input from professionals involved in someone's care. The national and local guidance is clear and comprehensive and is easy to find online.

Significantly, in 2019, the scheme changed to further include people with non-visible (or 'hidden') disabilities such as autism and anxiety disorders. Thus, the scheme widened to include people for whom access to public places was limited due to psychological distress, behaviour or a lack of situational awareness presenting a safety risk. The threshold for qualification is still reasonably high (the term 'very considerable difficulty' is used), but nevertheless, the changes represent important progress.

Further support

Government guidance
www.gov.uk/government/collections/blue-badge-scheme

Your own local authority's guidance

'Relaxed' sessions at museums and attractions

Access to public spaces and events can present many challenges for people with special needs. There are sometimes physical barriers such as tight spaces, and there are often environmental factors such as noise and busyness. Fortunately, however, progress has been made both in terms of awareness of others' needs and accessibility. Many museums, galleries and other attractions hold separate sessions for children with SEN. These are sometimes referred to as 'quiet' or 'relaxed' sessions. These sessions tend to be less busy and quieter (often background music or loud exhibits will be turned off), and staff and other visitors will expect to see atypical behaviour and be ready to offer extra help. Not only do these adaptations make things more accessible, they can also significantly reduce stress for parents!

Relaxed sessions tend to be fairly infrequent and are held early in the morning or late in the afternoon rather than at peak times, but the atmosphere is often particularly welcoming and friendly. It is a good chance to socialize with other children and families with similar needs, and even to meet new friends. The sessions tend to be free of charge (entry is free to public museums anyway), but you may need to provide evidence of your child's needs – such as an EHCP – and pay for entry to private attractions.

If somewhere you want to visit does not have a relaxed session, consider asking for one to be organized. You may need to point out other locations as examples or organize a lobby with other families you know. While it may be practically and financially more difficult for smaller locations to schedule special opening times, most will at least be willing to try to accommodate your needs. Indeed, they may have a legal obligation to do so on some level, in line with their duty to provide 'reasonable adjustments' for disabled people.

MAKING MUSEUMS ACCESSIBLE FOR OUR AUTISTIC SON

Stephen shares his own experience of attending a 'quiet session' at a museum with his son.

Like a lot of his peers, our autistic son is really keen on transport, especially the London Underground. He loves travelling on public transport, but for him, museums are far too overstimulating. He can't stand the number of people, the sensory overload and being told not to touch this or that or not to climb on all the exhibits. Unfortunately, the London Transport Museum is crowded and noisy and makes him feel really stressed really quickly. We would never normally go to that kind of environment with him, but we were invited a few years ago as part of a family trip. Sure enough, it was all too much for him, but he did really love the whole idea of a building full of trains and buses.

Luckily, we found out that the museum runs quiet sessions about every six months for children with SEND. Since our first visit, we have been back three other times, all of which have been successful. When you go to a quiet session, the pressure is really off, and he can wander around without us being worried he'll push into too many queues or get lost in a crowd. We always seem to bump into people we know, which is really nice.

The difference is amazing. What used to be a really stressful experience is now something we look forward to as a family. There's nothing quite like seeing all the autistic kids in transport heaven, reeling off facts about the underground or repeating phrases from the public address announcements to their hearts' content. It's a really joyful place on those mornings, where lots of children can relax and just be themselves.

Short breaks

It is well worth learning about your local authority's 'short breaks' offer. This will typically provide some kind of motivating and enjoyable activity for the child or young person while also providing some space and time for other family members. It could be a week-long, specialist holiday camp for disabled children; conversely, it might just be about your child attending a youth centre (or similar) so that you can do the weekly shop or get a haircut (which are both environments that can prove tricky for some children with SEND).

Further support

To find out more about what short breaks are available in your area, follow the link below / this QR code and enter your postcode

www.gov.uk/apply-short-term-care-for-child

Siblings and other family members

Tolstoy's epic family saga, *Anna Karenina*, begins with the famous statement that, 'All happy families are alike, each unhappy family is unhappy in its own way' (Tolstoy, 2016, p.3). You could say something similar for families of children with SEND; not that they're unhappy, but that they are all unique. Lamentably, there is no formula for helping siblings to get on. Common themes do emerge, however.

It's often reported that siblings of children with SEND mature more quickly because of their additional caring responsibilities. Conversely, they may also resent the additional attention their sibling gets. They may feel proud of their brother or sister, or they may feel embarrassed by them.

It's certainly true that the sibling of a child with SEND will often have a different experience of home life than a child in a family with no SEND. This is not something to feel guilt over, just something to recognize. The charity Sibs provides advice, networking and workshops for the siblings of children with SEND (with an offer for parents also). See the 'Further support' section for a link to its website.

SUCCEEDING AS A FAMILY IN THE CONTEXT OF SEND
Arabella and John share what family life looks like for them, including how they manage the sibling dynamic.

We have two sons, Benny and Freddie. Benny, who is older and autistic, is often prioritized over Freddie, who has some sensory issues but isn't autistic. I don't like how that sounds, but it's just the reality – the fallout if his needs go unmet is more extreme.

While this manifests itself in big ways, it also affects us in a multitude of smaller ways: not allowing our friends to stay later than planned on a Saturday afternoon, when a friend jokes with Benny but he doesn't get it or trying to eat out somewhere. These harmless social acts create a knock-on impact of either waking during the night for several hours or reduced capacity and ability to cope the following day. I call it a social hangover.

Parenting without judgement

Both boys have sensory issues around food; they don't like mixed textures. Freddie is very sensitive to smells and so often sits at a different table to eat dinner. They eat different things, which means making three different meals. This takes extra preparation, and to be honest, it gets wearing.

People have suggested I pander to them; they suggest I make one meal, and if they don't eat it, they go hungry. These types of comments irritate me and show such a lack of understanding of sensory issues. If I tried to force my children to eat the same thing, they would become distressed and dysregulated. They'd go to sleep hungry and night-times would be even more disrupted.

Making night-times work

Benny has a sleep disorder diagnosis, meaning he struggles to get to sleep and stay asleep. This has been hugely aided by the prescription of melatonin for the past 18 months. Prior to this, bedtime was almost always protracted over several hours, which was frustrating for all. We tried everything – bedtime involved massages, lights, weighted blankets, scents, baths, etc.; you name it, we tried it!

He essentially needed the melatonin. Now, most nights, he falls asleep well and the anxiety and knock-on emotional dysregulation is largely gone. Sometimes, accepting that there's something you can't 'parent through' is the best thing, no matter how hard that can be.

Siblings

The sibling dynamic can be challenging for all families. In ours, Freddie is currently picking up a lot of the complaining and negative responses as learned behaviour from Benny, especially around school and emotional regulation. However, more than anyone, Freddie helps show Benny how to love. Freddie is naturally very demonstrative and shows his love openly, demanding cuddles in a furious tone, and is not demotivated by Benny's lack of physical or emotional displays of love towards him. He has helped show Benny how to do this, and it's beautiful to watch. Freddie is also aware of his emotional needs and loves 'alone time' when 'feeling a bit overwhelmed' (his words), which is a gift from Benny too.

Perfectly imperfect

Whatever the situation in your household(s), muddling through is probably where you'll end up. Emotions often run high and then relent. One minute everyone is at each other's throats; the next minute they're sharing a joke. This can be amplified by a family member's additional needs – stress can run high, and things can feel helpless.

It's quite okay to recognize when things aren't easy and to get through them together. Be understanding, and don't judge your other children. They have a hard time and need to express and go through all their emotions as they grow up, learning that they will be loved anyway.

One of the many perfectly crafted, written and performed scenes in the BBC comedy series *There She Goes* illustrates familial relationships beautifully. The series follows the lives of a family of four with a neurotypical son and a daughter who has a learning disability and does not speak. It's based on the experiences of the creator and writer Shaun Pye, whose own daughter has a chromosomal disorder. During a family holiday, Rosie (the daughter) is constantly unsettled and wants to go home. She disrupts the planned activities, and everyone gets stressed. Ben (the son) gets more and more frustrated at missing out and having his own needs sidelined. He eventually erupts, crying angrily and shouting about how his sister ruins everything. His mum doesn't chastise him; she simply comforts him, recognizes his feelings and tells him it's okay to feel like that sometimes. In the very next scene, he is calm and he and his sister are happily playing together in the swimming pool (Pye, 2020). Being perfectly imperfect is one of the many themes of the series, and it should be recommended viewing for any family. All the characters have their ups and downs, not least Simon, the dad, who initially reacts to his daughter's disability by drinking too much and generally acting like an ass. But what ultimately binds the family is love, and it is this that makes the series so true to life.

Further support

Sibs – the charity for the brothers and sisters of disabled children and adults

www.sibs.org.uk

Special occasions

I'm not sure if it is possible to generalize about special occasions. For starters, each family is different and celebrates different things. For some, birthdays are no big deal; for some, religious festivals are the most important days of the year, etc. And children with SEND are probably as varied in how they react to special occasions as the occasions themselves. But there are a few comments to make.

If your child is sensitive to change and likes routine, they may be completely thrown by Christmas, Eid or whatever is celebrated by your family. In these cases, you may find that your family tones down the festivities and has a more limited change to routine.

You may of course not want to do this, and your child might need to get through as best they can. In that case, draw on the information in Chapter 3 about visuals and communication to prepare your child in advance. Try to think things through and plan, plan, plan. The less uncertainty the better. You might even decide to tell them in advance what presents will be in the wrapping paper or perhaps not use wrapping paper at all!

You might need to brief family members as to what to expect from your child. This is never easy, as inevitably some uncle or grandparent just won't get why the world seems to revolve around the sensibilities of a young child. But do what you feel is in everyone's best interests. You might feel like you need to juggle everyone's needs, and this can be stressful. I know one girl who will happily attend birthday parties but whose mother insists nobody sings 'Happy Birthday' because it makes her daughter cry and scream.

Some children who by rights *should* dislike surprises and parties absolutely love them. Our autistic son actually goes mad for anything with a kind of social ceremony. He adores going to Granny's for Easter egg hunts, loves 'pass the parcel' and 'trick or treat', and looks forward to Christmas. This is the same child who will be thrown out of step if we need to deviate from the usual route to school or if weekend plans change at short notice. Not everything follows a logical pattern. You will learn with your child as they grow up, and they will also probably change over time. Be responsive but balanced.

Stephen

SEND merchandize

There is a myriad of products available that are designed and/or marketed to help with SEND. Some are good and some are not. Most are somewhere in the middle. You could categorize them thus:

- Genuine tools to enable disabled people to carry out everyday tasks they would not otherwise be able to do. Examples include kettle tippers, walking aids and adapted cutlery.
- Aids that target a particular sensory challenge common in people with SEND. Examples include ear defenders, silicone chewing products and clothing without itchy seams.
- New inventions that have anecdotal evidence for their use but may also be novelty items. Examples include weighted blankets and jackets.[1]
- Refinements of existing toys or products supposedly optimized for people with SEND. Examples include fidget toys (which are like toys), sensory balls (which are like balls), etc.
- Poorer quality toys with some use that have the words 'sensory', 'fidget' or often 'Montessori' etc. slapped on them to try to make them more attractive to buy. Examples include spinning things, talking flashcards and light or bubble tubes, etc.

Some of the above can be really great additions to the toy box or

---

1   My apologies if these items are more than a novelty for you or your child.

school bag. My son spent a month chewing through all his school T-shirts when he had a wobbly tooth until we bought him a chew buddy. Problem solved. Others are just junk you can buy on Amazon marketed as 'SEND'.

Occupational therapists can advise on solving real-world issues. Your child's school might also have some experience with sensory challenges and with helping children to access learning if they are distracted or uncomfortable. But anything useful will probably be quite individual and will depend on what your child likes and needs.

More than anything, buy things when there is a real need, not just because they're for sale.

Routine

If our aim is for children to feel safe, happy and supported at home and at school, routine should be at the forefront of our thinking. Predictable routines make life easier for children and their families.

Routines work because they reduce uncertainty; and it is uncertainty that leads to anxiety. When children feel anxious – especially if they have difficulties communicating and understanding feelings – it leads to stress, tension and unhelpful behaviour. In extreme cases, this can lead to refusal to attend school or general demand avoidance. It can also increase stress for the rest of the family as parents and siblings struggle to help.

Needing to establish routines can feel depressing, especially if you live in the moment and thrive off spontaneity. But conversely, they can be quite liberating. Knowing that your child will be as calm and centred as possible is a big motivator. In time, you will also identify your child's tolerance for change. Inevitably, sometimes things don't go to plan, and it's impossible to control everything, but well-established routines can go a long way towards making life easier.

LEARNING THE VALUE OF ROUTINE (THE HARD WAY)
Stephen recalls a morning in which he underestimated how important routine is to his son.

We have a pretty well-established routine to get to school in the morning. First, I drop our youngest son at his school at 8:30 am and then our eldest at his (special) school, which starts at 9 am. It only takes 15 minutes to drive between each school, so we always arrive at the second school a bit early.

One day, I needed to get petrol, and I made the mistake of asking my son if we could go before I dropped him off. First, he said yes, but I don't think he knew it meant changing our route. When we started to drive to the petrol station, he freaked out and said he wanted to go to school. I quickly turned around and went to the school instead. But when we got there, he was really confused that we hadn't got the petrol yet. It was now nearly 9 am and time to go in, so I tried to hurry him out of the car so we weren't late. This made him more and more stressed until he eventually started having a mini meltdown outside the school gates about wanting to buy petrol. It didn't matter how much I tried to explain we no longer had any spare time.

Luckily, the headteacher is really understanding. She came out to see if she could help and I explained what had happened. She said, 'Look, just go and get the petrol and then come back.' So I did this, and he calmed down but was 15 minutes late for school. I won't make that mistake again!

What do we mean by routines and how can I establish them?

Some routine is inevitable in all our lives. We all need to eat regularly, sleep at night and try to do something vaguely productive in between.

If your child is struggling with emotional regulation or anxiety, putting in place more established routines is one of the first things to do to help. Routines can cover activities at home, such as bedtime, but can also be used for outings, such as supermarket shopping. The degree to which a daily routine needs to be prescriptive will vary from case to case. Here is an example of a simple morning routine:[2]

---

2   If any particular task in a schedule like this is in itself a challenge for your child, preparing a short social story or step-by-step instructions can help. A social story explains why a particular step is important (e.g., the importance of brushing your teeth to avoid tooth decay). See page 137. Step-by-step instructions can help with more complicated tasks until the various steps become second nature. For example, washing your hands involves turning on the tap, wetting your hands, applying soap and rubbing, rinsing, turning off the tap and drying. So many steps can be difficult to process. See page 135.

7 am: Wake up, toilet, get dressed
7:30 am: Breakfast
8 am: Wash face, brush teeth
8:15 am: Put on coat, shoes and school bag
8:30 am: Leave for school

Free time can be challenging for some children because of its unstructured nature. As such, having a regular weekend timetable can help.

During school holidays, you may be doing different things each day, but making sure you leave the house at the same time every morning establishes a daily rhythm and structure.

Take time to think of routines that you know are feasible and appropriate. Often less is more. Getting to the end of the day having completed a few planned activities with some downtime is better than trying to squeeze in extra activities if it results in you and your child feeling frazzled.

Once you have decided on the routine, preparing a visual timetable to communicate the routine to your child is always helpful. Indeed, it is helpful even if your child does not have any particular difficulty with processing verbal information. Visuals help reinforce what you are trying to get across, and the whole family can see them quickly and easily. In fact, I would argue they are beneficial for all children. See page 124.

USING ROUTINES TO BRING CALMNESS TO OUR DAY
Stephen shares how visual timetables can be used to support daily routines and reduce anxiety.

When I left work to stay at home and look after our two boys, they were three years old and ten months old. I had always been hands-on from the start, but nothing could have prepared me for looking after both of them full-time. Our eldest was probably going through one of his most challenging phases. He is autistic but was not yet diagnosed; he had very little language and instead communicated through screams, giggles and actions.

It's well established that sensory and cognitive differences can make the world seem overwhelming and confusing to autistic people. As a result, some autistic children try to control their environment to mitigate their anxiety. Our son had become very rigid in what he would and would not do. It's hard to describe to others how a two- or three-year-old could dictate what we did and where we went, but he must have been so unnerved by all the things he didn't understand about the world that he developed what are actually quite logical coping mechanisms.

For example, almost every afternoon, we had to walk to the nearby tube station and catch an underground train for one stop. We then alighted and caught an overground train – again, just for one stop. We would then walk down the high street, stop at Pret A Manger for a pot of mango, go to the playground opposite and then get the 206 bus home. Doing this with a baby in tow was really hard. I could not say, 'Please wait here for a minute while I feed your brother,' or, 'Can we skip Pret today because I can buy you two whole mangoes from Tesco for the same price?' He couldn't understand these things and would be triggered into acute stress.

After his autism diagnosis, establishing a daily routine and visual timetable was the single most useful and impactful thing we did at home. It helped to liberate us from my son's rigid habits and controlling behaviour. I used Velcro strips on the side of a kitchen cupboard to affix laminated pictures of all the things we scheduled each day. Once something was completed, my son could remove it and put it aside. This meant that each morning he knew what the plan for the day was and could always refer back to what was happening next. Having the timetable meant we could do a greater variety of activities and ensure important things like bath time weren't missed. We could incorporate new places – such as the dentist's – in advance, making it much less stressful all round.

Encouraging communication

If you, like me, have lost count of the times you've asked your child to 'use their words', you may need other ways for your child to communicate their wants or needs to you. Frustrating though it may be, pushing a child to use their words when they are dysregulated or anxious can create an additional anxiety about language, which can make matters worse. Removing the anxiety about speaking can be the most useful approach to encouraging language in the long term.

If you know there are times when your child struggles to communicate verbally, there are a few things you might try.

Non-verbal communication systems

You might try using a non-verbal communication system that uses visuals in order to ensure the child can have their communication needs met. This can be particularly effective for requests that require basic language. Does your child want a drink or a snack? Do they want to go outside or go to their bedroom? At its most basic level, it allows a child to tell you without using their words that they'd like an apple, are feeling sad or want to see Dad. It allows you to tell them, without having a reliance only on words, that they need to brush their teeth, that there are two different lunch options to choose from or that they will get a sweet *after* they've done their homework.

If you embed this as a system that the child uses when they are feeling calm and regulated, it won't add to the anxiety if you're encouraging the child to use it when they are dysregulated. The most common resource of this nature is the Picture Exchange Communication System (PECS), which describes both the resource itself and the method of using it. Starter packs are available for parents to buy online.

Talking Mats

Developed by SALTs, this visual communication tool allows children who are pre-verbal, or who struggle to express themselves verbally, to share their views on a range of topics relevant to their age and ability. Schools, especially SALTs, like using these to get a deeper level of understanding about a child's likes and dislikes. Without requiring high levels of language, they allow the child to share, for example, what they most love about school and what is harder for them, which types of support help them and which don't, etc.

Choosing the right moment

Many children struggle to use their words when they are dysregulated but use words well otherwise. If your goal is to encourage communication (e.g., about something they found upsetting), it may therefore be helpful sometimes to return to a moment of distress after the event. When children are dysregulated, they might genuinely find it impossible to use appropriate words or even to use any words. However, mentioning an event a bit later (and potentially in a light-hearted manner) can allow that child to express the thing that frustrated them without being in the heat of the moment. It can even give you the space to teach your child what a more appropriate response might be the next time they feel that way.

Parents' intuition

All the advice above has worth, but don't doubt your own intuition in relation to your children. A combination of parental instinct and trial and error will teach you when your child needs a hug, when they need to be left alone or when they need something else entirely.

Promoting independence

We all want our children to be as independent as they can be. For many parents of children with SEND, the fear about their child's ability to live independently as an adult is felt from a very early stage.

Dependence and independence are not two sides of a coin, of course. Independence usually happens slowly, sometimes seeming to move in reverse at times. To support your child on their long journey towards independence – in whatever aspect of their development – you might consider embedding some of the following day-to-day habits:

Present things visually

Where you feel yourself having to give (and perhaps repeat) instructions to your child every 15 seconds, particularly around the time pressure of a morning routine, try a visual approach. Rather than your verbal instruction being one of many things going through your child's head, a visual can be an effective communication tool that also frees you up as a parent (to get yourself/other children ready, for example!). See page 129 on how to create and use a visual timetable.

Transfer some ownership

As discussed on page 144, children are often more motivated with a task if they have some autonomy within it – if they feel it is theirs rather than yours. Where possible, involve your child in decisions around whatever you want them to be more independent about (choosing an outfit, unpacking the shopping, completing a piece of homework).

Don't always help too much

In a school context, research has shown that, in some cases, the more one-to-one adult support a child has, the less progress they make (Blatchford *et al.*, 2009).

It is perhaps easy to understand how children will do less for themselves when someone else will do it for them, whether we're thinking about decoding a word in Year 1 or getting themselves a cup of squash at home.

It's human instinct to help those we love; that instinct is stronger when we know our child finds certain aspects of their life difficult. But, by thinking not, 'What's the most I can do for my child?', and instead thinking (within the realms of their safety!), 'What's the least help my child needs here?', we can support our children to increase their independence over time.

Take advice

When speaking to therapists, clinicians or teachers, you will inevitably be looking to find out, 'What can I do? What help do they need?' Alongside this, try to develop a mindset of, 'What are we trying to support them to be able to do? What are the steps involved to make them more independent in relation to this (skill/task, etc.)?'

Challenging behaviour

'Challenging', in this context, has two meanings. Sometimes, your child's behaviour will be challenging. And sometimes, you need to challenge your child's behaviour.

As a parent, we all have things that particularly pull on our emotions, often frustrating us. Some will be deeply rational things we get annoyed by, whereas other things just seem to 'touch a nerve'. It might be that as parents we lose our temper, often to our children's amusement, when they do some of the following things:

- Continually tip things out of boxes or drawers, especially when you have just tidied them up.

- Pull books off bookshelves.
- Take off clothing.
- Refuse to wash/brush teeth/dress.
- Run across roads.

The list could go on: every child has their own unique and special way of testing our patience as parents.

You'll see that some of these behaviours are not only frustrating for parents, they are also actually dangerous for the child. If you are struggling with behaviour that puts your child or others in danger – for example, if they self-harm when they're stressed or touch others inappropriately – you might be able to get more help in dealing with it. A link is provided in 'Further support' at the end of this section.

You may find your child's behaviour frustrating if they're wired differently. You may also find it vexing just because they're a child and you're an adult. Either way, if they have special needs, dealing with it can be doubly difficult. If a neurotypical child misbehaves (or makes poor choices, depending on how you like to describe it) once in a while, raising your voice might be enough to nip it in the bud. But if your child behaves in ways that frustrate you – or even put them in danger – as a matter of course, you need to be much more strategic about supporting your child and managing your own emotions lest you get burnt out.

You need to react objectively and try to minimize your emotional connection to the issue. This is easier said than done, because as a parent you will be emotionally entwined with your little one at all times. But you need to step back sometimes and think critically. For a parent, the ability to regulate their own emotions, as well as their child's, is a key challenge – and it is one we all fail to meet at times.

Understanding behaviour

To start to understand behaviour, we need to look at its causes or functions. Sometimes, what's driving behaviour is self-evident, such as hunger, tiredness or excitement.

You need to be extra tuned into your child if they struggle to recognize and tell you how they're feeling. At other times, different things drive behaviour, which may be unique to your child. Hattersley (2013, p.13) lists four such reasons:

- Coping mechanisms to deal with unpleasant situations. *Example: Running away to avoid social situations.*
- Ways to manage sensory issues. *Example: Covering ears and screaming to block out certain noises.*
- A learnt behaviour that achieves a certain outcome. *Example: Screaming until you buy them an ice cream.*
- Something pleasurable. *Example: Smelling strangers' hair on the bus.*

When trying to deal with behaviour, remember that, ultimately, you don't have control over how your child acts: they have their own agency. You can shout until you are blue in the face, and it may not change anything. You have to think hard and sometimes accept that things won't go how you want. Dealing with behaviour is more like a constant dance between you and your child; it isn't a one-way street. Your job is to get to know your child inside out and to influence them in positive ways. If you find yourself regularly getting frustrated, take a step back and think about what's going on for them that might be causing this behaviour.

Beginning to change your child's behaviour
Think about what a particular behaviour's function may be and then tackle it at source. If your child is anxious, what is causing it? Or do they have an unidentified sensory need? Do they have strong feelings they have no other way of expressing? Has there been a change in routine, or is there something big on the horizon, like moving house or changing schools? You might also find it useful to make a (mental) note of the environment, time of day, etc. to help to identify patterns in their behaviour.

Use your detective skills to identify what you can change in the environment to make certain behaviour less likely. Help your child to do the same so they can begin to self-regulate. You might find yourself working on communication skills (see Chapter 3) to help your child express themselves. If you need to explain something, try using a social story (page 137). It's a cliché, but are they getting enough physical exercise and time to relax?

Try to avoid using rewards to stop a certain behaviour. While this may be very effective, it does not deal with any underlying issues and the problem may resurface. It can also send confusing messages to children. It isn't right to grow up thinking that your discomfort is only worth a star on a merit chart.

Remember, your child may not have the same potential as others to understand consequences or to know the impact of their behaviour on others. Empathy is often more appropriate than discipline, however hard that may be for you or people around you. Grandparents or indeed siblings may need to be educated in why you deal with behaviour in a certain way or appear less strict with one child than with another. That said, a passive acceptance of behaviour ('Oh, they don't understand') is almost as bad as blanket castigation. Every child deserves to learn what is right and wrong, but some just need to learn differently.

Further support

The Challenging Behaviour Foundation
www.challengingbehaviour.org.uk

CHAPTER 5

SUPPLEMENTARY THERAPIES

Not all children with SEND require therapy. Many people with SEND rightly point out that there is nothing to 'therapize' – to suggest that someone needs a certain therapy implies that there is something that needs fixing.

Other people will have experienced the transformative effect of a type of therapy themselves or have seen first-hand its effect on a family member.

In this chapter, we try to respectfully discuss the range of therapies that may be relevant when a child has SEND, although due regard is also given to the commercial interests and/or 'magic cures' that parents may need to consider with caution.

Early intervention?

If your child has been given a diagnosis, you may already have started researching treatments and therapies to help them. This is a perfectly natural reaction. You might not know what else to do but feel like you should be doing something.

First, don't rush into anything. Just because your child has a diagnosis, it does not necessarily mean they need anything fixing. The only thing that's different is that now they have a formal name for how they may differ from the norm.

It might feel like you need to act as quickly as possible so as not to miss a single moment to support your child; this is not really the case. Though there is typically a stress on 'early intervention' within

SEND, purveyors of treatments/cures can use 'early intervention' to play on parents' keenness to act or even perhaps their reluctance to fully accept the implications of a diagnosis.

'Treatments' are expected to begin as early as possible to have the greatest impact in the long term, and as such, it's possible for autistic toddlers to find themselves in 25–40 hours per week of behavioural therapy. Don't fall into this trap. Your child is exactly the same person as they were before the diagnosis, and there is no clock counting down to when it will be too late to help them.

Commercial interests

Be mindful of vested interests and attuned to the multitude of media used to market certain therapies and treatments that present themselves as objective. What might appear to be a neutral film or article may actually be promoting a certain viewpoint.

And though your child is to you the most precious thing there is, it may be that to some your child is a commodity and their condition an opportunity for profit.[1]

You should also be aware of certain 'health' industries' claims to 'correct' your child out of their condition. This seems to be a particularity of one way of understanding autism in America, and it's easy to find yourself being sucked into this way of thinking. You might hear claims that therapies can give your child a chance to become 'indistinguishable from their peers' or achieve 'normal intellectual and educational functioning'. But remember, you can't teach someone not to be autistic: it's part of who they are. It would be like trying to teach someone to have red hair instead of brown hair. You can dye it, but then you'd have a person with brown hair who has dyed it red, not a redhead. Any notion of 'treating' autism, Down's syndrome or dyslexia, etc. is contested. In and of themselves, they are ways of being, not illnesses to be cured.

The relative merits of therapy

It is true that many people with SEND have a harder time than others getting on in life and they often need extra help with things most

---

1   See Broderick and Roscigno (2021) for a discussion on neoliberal capitalism, disability as a commodity and people as its consumers.

people find relatively straightforward. But this doesn't always have to mean specialist therapy. There are many ways to help children to learn better, know themselves better, get on better – in short, to flourish. By joining sports clubs or learning a musical instrument, children can have fun, make friends, learn how to get on with others and develop physically. We don't call this kind of thing 'football therapy' or 'violin therapy', but the outcomes of taking part can be equally significant. The difference with therapy is the deliberate focus on certain outcomes and the additional skills and professionalism of practitioners. The difference this makes varies: many infants who struggle with communication catch up without the intervention of speech and language therapy, whereas for others this will be highly impactful.

It's worth thinking about the additional cost (both in terms of time and, often, money) of supplementary therapy. The time has to come from somewhere. What else would your child be doing were they not in therapy? They could well be learning other things anyway, academically and socially. Are they missing out on something at school, or will they have less time to play with their siblings or see family? If it's expensive, what else could you use the money for?

This is not to put you off seeking professional therapy. Far from it. Amazing transformations can take place with the right intervention. Unless there is an immediate need – like a health problem – don't rush into anything. It's up to you – and, to some extent, the professionals involved in your child's care – to decide if anything additional is required and is worth the additional energy (and perhaps money). But don't overload your child. Let them be most of the time. Enjoy family life. If they need a little extra help to be the best version of themselves, that's all good too.

Finally, do be aware of unproven and unsafe therapies and practices that do not have good regulatory systems and professional bodies. If in doubt, do your research and ask trusted professionals for advice. SENDCOs, doctors and registered professionals like speech therapists and occupational therapists are a good starting point.

Applied Behavioural Analysis

Applied Behavioural Analysis (ABA) is mainly, but not exclusively, used on autistic children. It is based on a kind of quasi-Pavlovian theory in which behaviour desired by the therapist is reinforced with rewards and undesirable behaviour is not: children get something they like in exchange for doing something else. It can be used to teach a variety of things such as life skills and communication. It is generally carried out in one-to-one therapeutic sessions but can also be integrated into general teaching to lesser or greater degrees. Therapists are normally certified by the UK Society for Behaviour Analysis or the Behavior Analyst Certification Board (BACB) (USA/international).

Despite these apparently benign parameters, ABA has the power to divide opinion, perhaps like nothing else in the world of SEND. Proponents argue that ABA can be pivotal in teaching important skills to improve autistic people's life chances, day-to-day living and potential for learning. Its proponents would say it's the most effective way to help autistic people. Its opponents, on the other hand, argue that it is theoretically flawed, ineffective and ethically questionable. Often arguments centre around whether autistic characteristics are differences to be embraced or deviations that require correcting. Critics also disagree with the focus on compliance over addressing the individual needs and desires of each child, and some people also think that skills learned during ABA therapy do not necessarily transfer to real-world situations.

There is a vocal lobby against ABA led, in many cases, by autistic self-advocates who were prescribed ABA as children and found the experience traumatic. They describe some of the methods – such as withholding rewards – as acutely stressful, especially if they were made to do things they found really hard or even painful, such as maintaining eye contact against their will.

In their forthcoming publication, *The Neurodiversity Affirmative Child Autism Assessment Handbook* (not yet published) Davida Hartman *et al.* summarize the neurodivergent communities' protests against ABA as follows:

> These approaches are fully rejected by the Autistic community and those working within the Neurodiversity Paradigm. Despite some recent reported industry changes and a great many kind and well-intentioned practitioners, ultimately the end goal of ABA is an Autistic young person and adult who meets neuro-normative assumptions such that they are 'indistinguishable' from their neurotypical peers.

Compliance-based behavioural methods (including PBS and ABA) have significant, negative, long-term effects on people's mental health (Anderson, 2022; Ram, 2020; Wakefield and McCarthy, 2020). They are incompatible with a human rights model emphasising the vital importance of self-advocacy and self-determination. If a method is based on compliance through behavioural means, it is not neurodiversity affirmative.

Proponents argue that ABA has evolved and now has less emphasis on coercion and a greater emphasis on building collaborative therapeutic relationships that address the needs of the individual.

If you are considering ABA for your child, you will need to draw your own conclusions. As with any other type of therapy though, its pursuit should not supplant the process of accepting your child for who they are. More often than not, the cost of private ABA therapy may be prohibitive anyway.

Further support

UK Society for Behaviour Analysis
https://uk-sba.org

Behavior Analyst Certification Board
www.bacb.com

Search online for voices from the autistic community and organizations arguing for/against ABA

Art therapy

Art therapy is all about using the creative process of self-expression as a way to approach emotional, psychological or communication challenges. Trained therapists facilitate participants to externalize thoughts and feelings and gain insight into them.

For children with SEND it can provide new ways to communicate, a different sensory experience and environment, help with social interaction and communication, support with emotional regulation and help to develop self-esteem and confidence. Its holistic and open-ended nature may not appeal to everyone, but skilled therapists will ensure it is personalized to optimize its benefits.

Further support

British Association of Art Therapists (BAAT)
https://baat.org

HCPC
www.hcpc-uk.org

Animal-assisted therapy

Animals are often employed for therapeutic purposes in schools and in external settings. Some schools have pets and in some cases they might be referred to as 'therapy dogs' or such like. The presence of animals can have a calming effect on emotions and help children to connect with how they're feeling; they can also help a child to recognize the agency of others. The sensory experience itself – connecting with warmth, softness, the outdoors, etc. – may be stimulating and beneficial. And children may develop their communication and social skills – while building confidence and trust – by working with therapists and alongside other children. There may also be opportunities for physical development of various kinds. Many children gain a great deal by learning to look after pets at home too by taking responsibility for their care.

Therapy with animals may be formalized in the same way as art or music – for example, equine therapy. In these cases, trained therapists will work with professional standards under supervision and often with goals in mind.

Animal-assisted therapy is not regulated by a single body in the UK so you should seek professional advice if you are trying to find out about it in your area.

Music therapy

Music therapy is a creative, engaging and flexible form of therapy where therapeutic relationships are developed through accessible music-making, interaction and reflection. It is an established clinical intervention with a protected professional title. Therapists are regulated by the Health and Care Professions Council (HCPC), and you can check their registrations on its website.

Music therapy sessions can include (but are not limited to) free improvisation, song writing, musical games and creative play. No prior musical experience is required, and sessions aim to develop the creative and communicative potential of whoever accesses them. This form of therapy can be particularly beneficial for those who experience barriers to communication, high levels of anxiety and social isolation. This includes people with physical and learning disabilities, SEN and mental health conditions.

Aims and benefits of music therapy vary according to the individual, but the therapeutic work often focuses on developing self-awareness, communication, concentration and attention skills. Through an experience of being understood, accepted and celebrated, music therapy can also improve underlying self-esteem, confidence and resilience.

Accessing music therapy

Music therapy takes place in certain mainstream and specialist settings, including settings for pupils with social, emotional and/or mental health needs, depending on the approach, values and funding capacity of the individual school. It is also available through the NHS as part of certain child development services, as well as in certain charities and at private practices.

Further support

British Association for Music Therapy
www.bamt.org

HCPC
www.hcpc-uk.org

THE VIEW OF A MUSIC THERAPIST

Hugh Anderson describes the benefits of music therapy for children and their families by telling us about the experience of a child he worked with.

Dakota began accessing music therapy sessions at our centre shortly before her fourth birthday and went on to access 16 sessions over a period of five months. In their referral, her parents expressed that they wanted to develop Dakota's potential for communication and interaction and to offer her opportunities to build her confidence and self-esteem. She had some areas of developmental delay, particularly in language.

Dakota quickly warmed to the music therapy environment, where there is a range of accessible instruments and sensory resources, and she appeared to be excited and impatient to start sessions each week. Her parents were both present in the room and gave her space to explore whilst being available if she needed reassurance or support.

Adapting to Dakota

Dakota was generally very independent and self-directed in her play, moving between different instruments and different parts of the room at her own pace, and it was sometimes hard to reach her. The nature of sessions shifted from week to week as I adapted to Dakota's varying engagement, mood and needs, but my fundamental aims remained consistent:

- To find a way of connecting with Dakota, however she presented on a given day, and to model a sense of acceptance and understanding.
- To celebrate Dakota's personality and facilitate an open, non-threatening space for her to express herself in different ways.
- To use music and play as tools for developing interaction and communication between Dakota and myself, as well as with her parents.

Sometimes, I would initiate familiar songs that we could all join in with and that I could adapt (by changing lyrics, speed, mood, etc.) to maximize her understanding and engagement. At other times, I would use music to match the rhythm and energy of Dakota's play and movements, acting as a witness and validator of what she was doing. I would also use music to accompany more reflective and tender moments when Dakota sought physical contact and connection with her parents.

Overall, Dakota and her parents appeared to have a very positive experience of music therapy. I witnessed many encouraging signs of development in her confidence, resilience and communication. Dakota maintained a very curious and enthusiastic approach and seemed to revel in a consistent, therapeutic space that she could make her own.

Having sessions with her parents present also gave the family a unique experience of being with one another and playing together. We talked about different kinds of songs and interactions from music therapy that could be facilitated in the home environment, with the hope that our work together could have a positive impact on family interactions in the long term.

Occupational therapy

The NHS website (2023b) says that OT 'aims to improve your ability to do everyday tasks if you're having difficulties.'

In relation to their work with children and young people, an occupational therapist might do any of the following things:

- Write a fine motor skills programme, typically increasing control of fingers or hands – a handwriting programme, for example.
- Write a gross motor skills programme, typically increasing control of arms or legs – throwing, running, catching a ball, etc.
- Support a child's independence, perhaps by writing a programme that helps them to dress themselves or use the toilet.
- Advise on the use of assistive technology.

It can be tricky in some parts of the country to get your child in front of an occupational therapist. Much will depend on their age and level of need, with children often needing to have numerous functional difficulties if they are to meet the criteria for referral.

If you think your child requires assessment from an OT, ask your school SENDCO or GP about referral processes in your area.

Rebound therapy

Rebound therapy was formulated in the late 1960s, by Eddy Anderson, and incorporates the use of trampolines for students on a wide spectrum of neurodiversity.

It can have many benefits for a whole range of children with SEND. It can enable children with all types of disabilities to strengthen their core; it can encourage spatial awareness; it can improve muscle tone, balance, relaxation, coordination of limbs and fitness; it can help to improve communication skills and develop kinaesthetic awareness.

Anyone can be encouraged to participate. For sensory issues, there are many tools that you can use to enhance the experience. Special mats, parachutes, fitness balls and rollers are just some of the aids that allow the participants to experience different sensations and to use their senses, touch, sight and hearing. Instructors can also adapt the way they communicate and teach for children who struggle to process spoken language.

COMING A LONG WAY WITH REBOUND THERAPY
Caroline Quist describes how a young child's development was supported with regular trampolining sessions.

Nigel attended my rebound therapy sessions at the age of seven. He was a pre-verbal child with Angelman syndrome, a genetic disorder that affects the nervous system. Those with Angelman syndrome tend to have developmental and intellectual disabilities, and balance and movement problems. Some can have seizures and disrupted sleep patterns.

It took Nigel's mother three weeks to get him to even enter the sports hall. When he eventually approached the trampolines, he was wearing a protective helmet in order to prevent head injuries because of his unstable gait.

After another four weeks of encouragement, we then made the decision to lift him onto the trampoline, as he was unable to coordinate his limbs to do this himself. He could not stand up on the trampoline at first, so I sat behind him and bounced with him, rocking him backwards, forwards and sideways. This went on for a number of weeks. I eventually got him to his feet and held his hands and gently bounced him, so he could experience being weightless. The expression on his face was pure joy.

Nigel attended the sessions regularly for about four years, gaining a lot more confidence, and was able to balance on his own and to let go of my hands. As he was pre-verbal, I had to use a lot of sign language/ word association. The word "bounce" was verbalized by me often and accompanied with signing.

On one particularly memorable occasion, and totally unexpectedly, Nigel said the word 'bounce'. This was Nigel's first word ever uttered in any situation. You can imagine the impact this had on me and also the rest of the class. We were all in tears. I nominated Nigel for a local award that year and he won 'Sports Personality of the Year'.

Nigel is now 22 and still enjoys his bounce therapy sessions each week. It is such a gift to be able to teach this incredible therapy.

Speech and language therapy

The Royal College of Speech and Language Therapists (n.d.) says that SALTs, 'assess and treat speech, language and communication problems in people of all ages to help them communicate better.'

'Speech, language and communication needs' is the most commonly reported form of SEND in English schools. While not all those pupils will need direct, long-term support from a SALT, there will be many who find that this type of support transforms their ability to make themselves understood or to access a school curriculum.

When working with children, SALTs typically cover the following areas:

Speech

Where children have difficulty making certain speech sounds, a block of therapy would help the child to form the correct shape with their mouth, to use their tongue and lips to support them to make the right sound, etc.

Language

A block of therapy focused on language development might support a child with their receptive language skills (i.e., to take meaning from the things they hear), their expressive language skills (i.e., how they communicate through speech) or both.

Communication

Some SALTs will support children with social communication difficulties who may or may not have a particular diagnosis. A block of therapy in this area may support a child to understand non-verbal cues, to consider their own body language or to take turns in a conversation or game.

Swallowing

Where children (typically with physical disabilities) need support with eating, drinking and swallowing, it will be a SALT who supports the child by developing a support plan for them.

Access to speech and language therapy is determined according to a child's age, their level of SEND, etc. but is also highly varied across the country. Direct contact with a SALT is more likely if the child is younger, due to the benefits of early intervention in this area, or if they have an EHCP, due to the statutory nature of these documents.

For many children with speech and language needs, it may be that the initial assessment is completed by a SALT but the block of intervention is delivered by someone else – a speech and language therapy assistant at a clinic or a teaching assistant in a school, for example.

If you think your child needs to be either assessed or supported by a SALT, speak to your school's SENDCO or speak to staff at your child's nursery to ascertain whether referral is best made from yourself as a parent or through the school/nursery.

Talking therapies

For children with some forms of SEND, the opportunity to speak to someone professionally can help them to better understand their place in the world, can help them to manage their emotions more positively or can help them to consider how to establish and sustain successful relationships.

Here are some of the most common forms of talking therapy:

- **Cognitive behavioural therapy (CBT)**: This approach looks at events in the child's life and how they respond to them. It will look to support the child towards more positive responses to such events, exploring how a different set of thoughts, beliefs and actions can lead to a more positive outcome.
- **Counselling**: The child or young person will usually have a series of sessions, often delivered one-to-one, in which the counsellor explores some of the problem areas within the child or young person's life – whether relational, emotional or something else entirely.
- **Psychotherapy**: This may be offered when difficulties have lasted for some time and/or when they are quite severe. They may support a child who is experiencing anxiety or depression (NHS, n.d.).

See the Young Minds website for more information on these and other types of talking therapies.

Though private options are possible for some families, these services are typically also available (subject to thresholds, waiting lists, etc.) on the NHS. They are typically offered through CYPMHS clinics (also called 'CAMHS' clinics in many areas). To find your nearest CYPMHS clinic, the NHS has a search tool (see the 'Further support' section at the end of this section), or you could speak to your child's school or your local GP.

WORKING WITH CHILDREN WITH EMOTIONAL NEEDS

Vicky Cooke tells us about the importance of an open mind, and simple approaches, when working as a therapist.

As a professional working with children and young people on a one-to-one basis around relationships and trauma, I would note often that what was written about them in the referral would be a completely different experience upon meeting them. What became clear to me was how I could not judge or place projections, opinions or views, including sympathy, onto them but instead give them the space to simply be, which supported them to feel empowered within.

More specifically, I realized that if they feel that there are no impositions in the form of projections, judgements, opinions or views cast onto them, then they feel that they have full permission to be themselves, and as a result, they are more settled and less anxious.

Giving a space for children to be themselves

To have settlement in the body is to feel at ease within, and with, the environment around us. Settlement is experienced when we are given the space, and give ourselves the space, to be who we truly are from our innermost Essence, and when we don't succumb to external pressures or demands to be different, more or something in particular for someone. When we are truly settled, we feel complete.

Often, we can see emotional needs as being complex and so we may feel that working with a child should be complex as well. However, in my personal experience, this is not the case, and instead simplicity is the key. It has become very clear to me that the foundation of any work with a child stems first from my relationship with myself and then my connection and relationship with them. How open and at ease I am in myself allows them to feel they can be the same.

Supporting children to move forward

Barriers with words or understanding could be overcome by using pictures, making scrapbooks and building something they could take with them after the intervention. They can then look at them with their parents or guardians after the session.

When creating such things, each is adapted differently for each child, depending on what they need. Reflecting on the scrapbooks supported them to feel the different marker they have felt within their body and with the relationship with themselves, from the sessions, supporting them to move forward in life from a different space.

Further support

Young Minds – for more information about talking therapies for young people

www.youngminds.org.uk/parent/parents-a-z-mental-health-guide/counselling-and-therapy/#Commontypesof talkingtherapies

Find your nearest CYPMHS/CAMHS clinic

www.nhs.uk/service-search/other-health-services/child-and-adolescent-mental-health-services-camhs

Accessing therapy

Parents frequently struggle to know where to start. They may not know whether the child should even be receiving a course of therapy, let alone which type of therapy service to engage or where to find such a therapist. It can be really tricky.

As mentioned in the introduction, start with trusted professionals:

- If your child is in a nursery or school, speak to the SENDCO.
- If you have a close relationship with your family GP, go and see them.
- If your child has undergone a multidisciplinary assessment, seek advice from the lead practitioner involved (e.g., a paediatrician). It's often invaluable to seek out advice from local parents, but it's also essential to ensure that a professional has recommended that particular course of therapy for your child.

There are some types of therapy that a school is well placed to refer to. Depending on where you live, a school may well have a referral pathway to a speech and language therapy service, an OT service or a CYPMHS. Though these services appear to be overrun in many parts of the country, speak to your child's school to find out what is best.

CHAPTER 6

SUPPORT FOR PARENTS AND SIBLINGS

In this chapter, we will look at some of the supports that can make such a difference to families. The first of these is financial, with some advice on how to claim the benefits you are entitled to claim in many cases.

We then share some sources of information and advice. In addition to the QR codes and weblinks shared throughout the book, in this chapter we share some websites, books and social media accounts that might be useful in your pursuit of the information most useful and relevant to your child.

We start with an account from a parent who went on their own journey of SEND assessment and diagnosis, following the catalyst of his son's experience in the school system.

PURSUING A DIAGNOSIS AS AN ADULT

John speaks openly about the process of getting a diagnosis as an adult, including making the difficult decision to do so.

I remember when my wife first gently suggested that I might be autistic. I was making a cup of tea. It is a moment that still sticks in my memory.

Our son was six years old and struggling in Year 1. We had started looking into an autism diagnosis for him but it had never occurred to me that I might be autistic as well. Yes, my experience of primary school had been equally horrific and scarring and I should have recognized the similarity, but, like many autistic people, I assumed that it was because I was a bad kid and hid my shame VERY deep down in my soul.

After going down a research rabbit hole (one of my superpowers) I was stuck in a middle ground, both wracked with uncertainty and feelings of 'don't make a fuss' but undeniably recognizing that it fit; it made sense.

Diagnosis as an adult

I ultimately knew that I wanted to pursue a diagnosis, mainly for the confirmation and validation. I am a product of an upbringing where you didn't show fallibility or anything that marked you out as different, so a diagnosis gave me (literally) the certificate of authenticity, and I could get on with my life.

The process of a diagnosis was reasonably painless. The doctor asked me the same questions I'd been reading online and then referred me to a local specialist clinic to be diagnosed. I didn't hear anything for around ten months, but once I reached the top of the list, the process took around two months. I answered another set of the same questions, in another screening, but then was assessed over Zoom by the most wonderful psychologist. She was insightful, respectful, gentle and above all – positive. I remember her saying at the end, 'Congratulations, you're autistic,' and while it was mainly relief I felt at the time, looking back now I tear up with joy when thinking how it felt.

Self-acceptance

So then started the long journey of understanding and acceptance. I always liken it to finding out you're adopted – you are still the same person with the same values, likes and dislikes, but there's another part of you that you never knew about, and its existence touches every part of you and your experiences. It is a monumental task to unpack all of this, and for a long time, everything you do and think about will be viewed through the new lens of autism. It's like a coat – you try it on and you take it off; you ignore it and then come lovingly back to it; you sometimes feel conspicuous in it, and other times you dance around in it as free as a bird. It's a very weird, personal and unique experience.

Claiming Disability Living Allowance

In England and Wales, DLA for children is a weekly allowance for supporting a child under 16 who has difficulty walking or needs much more care than a child without a disability. The rate depends on the child's needs, and it ranges (at the time of writing) from £28.70 to £184.30 per week.

There are two elements to DLA – the care component and the mobility component – and your child may qualify for one or both of the components. The care component has three tiers of support (lower, middle and higher), and the mobility component has two tiers (lower and higher).

The care component ranges from 'help for some of the day' to 'help and supervision throughout both day and night'.

The lower mobility rate is for children who 'can walk but need help or supervision when outdoors'; the higher rate is for children who 'cannot walk, can only walk a short distance without severe discomfort, or are blind or severely sight impaired' (UK Government, n.d.(c)).

DLA is awarded on a needs basis and is not dependent on a diagnosis. If your child meets the criteria and doesn't have, or is waiting for, a diagnosis, you can still apply. Likewise, just because your child has a diagnosis, it doesn't necessarily mean they would qualify for DLA.

There are additional restrictions and exemptions to this summary of the guidance, and the whole thing can seem quite confusing at first; luckily, the government guidance is clearly written and accessible. See this guidance via the QR code or weblink below.

Applying for DLA

To apply for DLA, you must fill in and send off a form. It is quite long and can be quite daunting. Be prepared to spend some time on the form, and remember that the person reading it will not know your child and therefore you should be as thorough as possible when answering each question.

There are various ways to get help with the form. There is a government helpline, you could ask your child's SENDCO or other parents and some charities such as Citizens Advice and Contact also offer support.

Further support

Government guidance
www.gov.uk/disability-living-allowance-children

Citizens Advice
www.citizensadvice.org.uk/benefits/
sick-or-disabled-people-and-carers/
disability-living-allowance

Contact
https://contact.org.uk/help-for-families/
information-advice-services/benefits-financial-help/
disability-living-allowance

Claiming Carer's Allowance

If you care for your child, who is receiving certain benefits, for at least 35 hours per week, you could be able to claim the weekly Carer's Allowance of £81.90 at the time of writing (check www.gov.uk for the latest amounts). For example, you qualify for Carer's Allowance automatically if your child is eligible for the middle rate of DLA. Details of all the eligibility criteria can be found online via the QR code or weblink below.

In addition to the weekly payment, there are other advantages to claiming Carer's Allowance, such as automatic National Insurance credits (meaning you do not miss out on National Insurance contributions because you are not working). There are also restrictions and limitations: for example, you must earn less than £196 per week on average to claim Carer's Allowance. The online guidance is comprehensive but can be confusing because of how benefits and tax are intertwined. There are charities you can approach for help, such as Citizens Advice and Carers UK.

Further support

Government guidance
www.gov.uk/carers-allowance

Citizens Advice
www.citizensadvice.org.uk/benefits/
sick-or-disabled-people-and-carers/carers-allowance

Carers UK
www.carersuk.org/help-and-advice/financial-support/
carers-allowance

Claiming other benefits as a young person with SEND

As your child approaches adulthood, they may be eligible for a Disabled Students' Allowance or an Access to Work grant. See pages 121–122 for more information on these schemes.

Support with housing

If your house or flat is not suitable for your family and you do not have the means to procure what you need, you may be entitled to help. If you are looking for social housing, each local authority has different (although in practice not entirely dissimilar) criteria for deciding to whom to allocate its limited stock of council or housing association properties. Check with your own local authority. If you are already on a housing waiting list, you should make sure the council knows everything about your circumstances.

If you need to make adaptations to your existing home, you may be entitled to a Disabled Facilities Grant. These grants can be quite substantial – up to £30,000 in England – but are means tested. They are also available for landlords and if you are renting a property. To check all the rules, visit the webpage below.

Further support

Disabled Facilities Grants
www.gov.uk/disabled-facilities-grants

Check information with your own local authority

PARENTING A THREE-TIMES EXCEPTIONAL BLACK CHILD WITH SEND

Linnette tells us about her own journey parenting her son Phineas, who has three SEND diagnoses. She tells us about the positive qualities she's seen in herself while doing so.

Parenthood is an intricate tapestry woven with a myriad of emotions – worry, fear, annoyance – but at its core, it is fuelled by an enduring and unwavering love. As a parent, you gaze upon your child, recognizing the divine potential that lies within them.

You yearn for the world to witness their brilliance. However, when you know that your child's development may deviate from the norm, a profound realization settles: your child may require additional support to thrive in this world.

Moving from denial to strength

Every step of the journey, from the first joyful scans to the miraculous birth, fills your heart with hope and anticipation. You witness your child's milestones – speaking at nine months, walking at ten months – with pride and joy, only to face unexpected challenges as time passes.

In our case, amidst a cacophony of voices reassuring us that everything was fine, we grappled with refusals to assess for need, endless battles for speech therapy and enduring the torment of our child's screams and desperate pleas for help during the isolating times of lockdown. It is through these trials and tribulations that we found the strength to pursue a private assessment, finally shedding light on our child's journey with three diagnoses and a host of sensory needs, affirming that his care will be lifelong.

SEND, ethnicity and judgement on my child

As a mother of a child who is three-times exceptional and a Black male, my path became an arduous battle, strewn with societal obstacles. It became evident that society no longer viewed my child as an innocent young boy but rather as an adult, laden with preconceived notions and biases.

You reminisce about carefree walks, observing your child at age nine, donning his hoodie on a chilly day, simply enjoying the freedom of running around, only to be confronted with the piercing comments of those passing by, branding him a hoodlum.

Advocacy beyond SEND

I realize that my role extends beyond securing the necessary support for my child's SEN. I advocate for equitable treatment across all aspects of my child's identity, recognizing the interplay between race, disability and the need for social justice.

It's an ongoing journey, one that demands unwavering resilience, fortitude and a steadfast commitment to justice.

I see my experience as a call to action, urging society to recognize and embrace the multifaceted identities of individuals with SEND and to foster an inclusive environment where every child, regardless of their unique circumstances, can thrive and soar and live life in all its fullness.

Sources of information and advice

The aim of this book has never been to provide everything that parents need to know. Knowing this limitation, and knowing that the journey within SEND for many parents can be a lonely one, you might want to consider the following:

The Independent Provider of Special Education Advice

Understanding the legal rights of you and your child in relation to SEND can be complex, not to mention expensive. The excellent IPSEA website removes much of the mysticism here and is used extensively by both families and professionals. Take a look at some of the 'Quick Guides' to learn about EHCNAs, SEN transport and access arrangements.

IPSEA's 'Quick Guides'

www.ipsea.org.uk/pages/faqs/category/quick-guides

The Special Educational Needs and Disability Information Advice and Support Service

Every local authority has its own SENDIASS, but it's important to note that these services are independent of the local authority. The mission of these services is to provide support to parents and young people, where they request it, that is relevant to SEND. This will include support of a parental application for EHCNA (the process of trying to get an EHCP). Details of this service can be found on the relevant local authority's Local Offer website or by searching online for SENDIASS and the relevant local authority.

The Family Action website

Basic information for families in relation to SEND, as well as multiple links to a range of services, has been collated on the Family Action website. The website also contains details of the 'Family Line', a helpline for parents.

Family Action
www.family-action.org.uk

Books relating to SEND

The literature in relation to SEND is extensive. Be prepared to be surprised and challenged but to come out the other side a little more enlightened. Depending on your own experiences with SEND and depending on the needs of your child, the following may be useful.

Raising Children: Surprising Insights from Other Cultures by David F. Lancy (2017)

This book synthesizes the author's career-long anthropological research into childhood in a highly accessible format designed for parents. Though not directly about SEND, it helped me to consider why I (Stephen) was making the decisions I was making about bringing up a baby.

Far from the Tree by Andrew Solomon (2012)

This book looks at the experience of raising a child who has a difference of some kind – be it deafness, Down's syndrome, autism (and other chapters not relating to SEND). Based on hundreds of parent interviews, it is excellent. It's also nearly a thousand pages long, but it's well worth a read if this is the level of detail you're looking for.

The Reason I Jump by Naoki Higashida (2014)

This book is written by a pre-verbal autistic 13-year-old, explaining their own experience of being autistic. It's a window into the world of someone who has so much to say and which most of us lack the skill to hear.

Supporting Your Child with Special Needs: 50 Fundamental Tools for Families by Rachel R. Jorgensen (2023)

This practical book looks at how parents connect with their child, with their child's school and with themselves as a parent. It contains sensible messages and has some useful templates throughout. Though much of the advice is useful, as it's written by an American author, much of the school context needs to be interpreted slightly in order to have relevance in the UK.

The Continuum Concept by Jean Liedloff (1975)

This fascinating book, based on the author's research from an indigenous community in Venezuela, seeks to understand human behaviour and child-rearing through the perspective of evolutionary theory. It isn't an academic book though – it's very much written for parents.

A Different Kind of Perfect: Writings by Parents on Raising a Child with Special Needs by Cindy Dowling, Neil Nicoll and Bernadette Thomas (2006)

This book is to be recommended if you are looking for personal accounts written by parents who may be on a similar journey to you.

100 Ways Your Child Can Learn Through Play by Georgina Durrant (2021)

If you're looking to develop your child's learning, particularly where it feels like formal learning is not the right approach for home, look at

Georgina's book, full of practical ideas. Georgina is a former SENDCO, so there is much in there that has relevance for parents of children with SEND.

Toilet Training and the Autism Spectrum by Eve Fleming and Lorraine MacAlister (2016)

Although this book is aimed at professionals or parents of autistic children, it is also useful to any parent who needs extra support with toilet training.

More books are listed in the bibliography.

THRIVING AS A FAMILY

Andy and Carys talk about what they have learned along the way so that they can succeed as a family.

The day we received our son Freddie's ASD (autism spectrum disorder) diagnosis, the paediatrician gave us a leaflet from the National Autistic Society and sent us on our way. Over the past eight years, we have collected a number of other diagnoses and been met with much the same response each time – here is a diagnosis, have a leaflet and crack on with it.

We were surprised at the lack of support available over the years and have found that our greatest sources of strength and support have been other parents with children similar to Freddie. We are part of a group run by a local children's charity and they accept us as the quirky family we are.

The needs of the sibling

Something we wish we had considered sooner is the impact of Freddie's complex needs on his younger brother, Charlie. It really helps us to engage with the family worker at Charlie's school, as it gives him someone to talk to about how he is feeling and a safe space where he can be honest about how he is finding things.

Registering with 'Young Carers' has also been great, as it helps the sibling see that they are not the only one coping with challenges at home and that there are friendships to be made with others who understand.

Working out what we need to succeed

It has taken us a long time to recognize what works for us as a family and to put our needs first. For so long, we tried to do 'normal' things with our extended family, to keep everyone happy, but they never knew how to help or what to do when it was too overwhelming.

We now know it is okay to say when something will not work for us, and after a long time, we no longer feel guilty about doing so. After years of not wanting to burden friends with the reality of how tough things can be, and constantly replying, 'We're fine!' when asked, we have learnt to share a little and can see how it helps.

We are definitely not the same people we were before we had Freddie, but we have muddled through. Remember, it is okay to be vulnerable; it is okay not to be okay.

Social media

We've all been lost down the social media rabbit hole. However, we've also been able to use it to find people outside our immediate social circle who have useful shared experiences, as well as to find expert advice.

Facebook

With a quick search, you can easily find groups on Facebook dedicated to everything under the sun. If you look at the number of members, you quickly get an idea of which are the most prolific.

Some Facebook groups are excellent online communities and host useful resources; they also have their limitations. If you're looking for mutual support, they can be great. You can find like-minded people and share stories and experiences. If you're looking for objective information and advice, you need to remember that most groups come about because of a particular idea and are administered by people who regulate the content. They can become echo chambers.

If the administrators are ideologically motivated, this can mean very one-sided information and, in the worst cases, shaming and bullying of people who differ from the accepted views. Oftentimes quite innocent questions from concerned parents can incur a strong response from group members who take offence at 'uninformed' views.

So take everything with a pinch of salt, avoid confrontation and know when to duck out.

Twitter/X

On Twitter/X, you might choose to follow some of the following to hear directly from those who either have SEND, parent children with SEND or advocate/carry expertise in relation to SEND:

@SpcialNdsJungle
@sos_sen
@SendHelp_UK
@IPSEAcharity
@SendCrisis
@PhoenixEdSarah
@commaficionado
@higashidanaoki2
@CDC_tweets
@Ellise_Hayward_

GETTING DIAGNOSED YOURSELF – AND WHAT TO DO WITH YOUR DIAGNOSIS

John shares his thoughts on how to approach your own diagnosis as an adult for the good of yourself and those around you.

Receiving a diagnosis of autism as an adult can cause issues. Partners and friends have no real reference point and can find it hard to understand or support you. The whole thing can also slightly blow a fuse in your brain, and many people go through 'autistic burnout'. I personally had a pretty nasty breakdown, which took time to process and left significant scars in my marriage. I wouldn't say not to go through a diagnosis – probably just do it better than I did.

Things that I recommend while going through this journey:

- Counselling – it's physio for your mind and worth every penny.
- Acceptance – this is a serious diagnosis and demands respect.
- Time – this can be a hard one for autistics, as we want to flick a

switch and it all be okay, but these things take time to develop and permeate, so be patient.

- Kindness – to yourself and to your loved ones.
- Honesty – you've been masking for your entire life and are used to trying not to say anything inflammatory, but as long as you're respectful and sensible, then being honest with others (and yourself) is always going to help understanding, even if the honest answer sometimes is, 'I don't know how I feel.'

Know thyself

You've probably come to this point through a diagnosis of one of your children, so you owe it to them to take this seriously and get yourself sorted – you are a role model for your child, and you want to show them that it's okay to be vulnerable and honest with yourself.

The only thing to consider is timing. Can you and your family cope with your diagnosis at the same time as your child is going through one? It's worth thinking about how to mitigate the effect of multiple diagnoses – should you move house or job while this is happening? Probably not, unless it's going to relieve a lot of stress. Should we skip date night? No, date night is non-negotiable. It's a stressful time; don't add to the already weighty pressure being exerted.

Owning your diagnosis

It's worth remembering that being autistic doesn't mean you can't do things; it's just that your cup of energy is used up faster by some things than others (or not used up doing others – give me a spreadsheet and I'll show you a happy autistic). A diagnosis doesn't tell you who you are or what you can and can't do; it just helps you understand why you find some things harder than others.

The great mind-scrambler is that you will likely very much enjoy many of the things you find exhausting (like socializing), but you just need to learn how to do them in a way that doesn't break you. You can do anything you want to, be anything you want to – you just need to learn the best way for you to do it.

Love and be loved, and the best of luck.

A NOTE BEFORE
WE LEAVE YOU

Thank you for reading this far – we're delighted that you have.

We hope the book has met the intended aim – to provide practical and relevant support across a broad range of areas relevant to your child's life, whatever their needs.

We hope it's met the intended tone – one of enormous respect for the hardworking and loving families who factor their child's needs into the hundreds of decisions they make every day.

And finally, we hope it's met the intended outcome – that in reading this book you have a greater sense of what others are doing, what the system entitles you to and what the future might just look like.

Glossary

Many of the terms in this book are best explained within the context of the sections they're most relevant to. We've therefore tried to introduce new terms throughout the book, for example, in Chapter 1, 'Definitions, Diagnoses and the Education System'. Here are some terms we might have missed and may also be useful.

Additional learning needs – This is used as the preferred term in Wales rather than 'special educational needs', which is the preferred term in England and Northern Ireland. In Scotland, the preferred term is 'additional support needs'.

Age-related expectations – In primary settings, all pupils are measured against the attainment typically expected by a given age, which is called 'age-related expectations'. In relation to this benchmark, parents will typically be told that their child is 'working above', 'working at', 'working towards' or 'working below'. For a pupil with SEND, this benchmark may very well be realistic for them, but if it isn't, the school may have another way of measuring their progress using descriptors more closely matched to the child's current attainment level.

CYPMHS – A Children and Young People's Mental Health Service provides, as you would expect, services to support the mental wellbeing of pupils, typically at a 'Tier 3' level – a level above that normally provided within or by schools. These are sometimes also called CAMHS (Children and Adolescent's Mental Health) clinics.

DSM-5 – This is shorthand for the 'Diagnostic and Statistical Manual of Mental Disorders, Fifth Edition', which lists many types of SEND. Though it is an American diagnostic manual, its definitions feature heavily once you get a little deeper into the literature on many types of SEND.

Education, Health and Care Plan (EHCP) – This is the term used for a document that many children and young people with higher levels of need will have. It outlines their needs, provision and the outcomes that should be in place for them, amongst other things. For more information on these, see page 74.

Emotionally Based School Avoidance (EBSA) – This is the term commonly used to describe a child who is not attending school. The term 'avoidance' is typically preferred to 'refusal', as it removes the insinuation that the child is actively refusing to attend.

Engagement Model – This is the statutory assessment framework used for pupils who are working far below the national curriculum. Recognizing that engagement with the learning is a fundamental stepping stone, it tracks progress against five related criteria – exploration, realization, anticipation, persistence and initiation.

Exam access arrangements – This is the term used to describe additional support given to pupils during examinations in order to remove a disadvantage that they might otherwise have, for example, due to a slow writing speed or difficulties with attention and focus. More details on such arrangements can be found on page 70.

Graduated Approach – If you read up about schools and their approach to meeting the needs of pupils with SEND, you'll come across this phrase. It refers to schools providing the right support at the right time, based on a four-part cycle of 'Assess-Plan-Do-Review'. Work out what the child needs, work out what to do about it, intervene appropriately and check if it works.

Higher level teaching assistant (HLTA) – This typically describes a teaching assistant with an additional responsibility (for leading interventions, for liaising with parents, etc.). Many HLTAs will have gained a specific Level-3 qualification in order to obtain this role. In some schools, the same job might be called a deputy SENDCO or assistant SENDCO.

ICD-11 – This is shorthand for the International Classification of Diseases, 11th Revision. It is a manual used by clinicians in the UK as the standardized criteria by which many types of SEND will be diagnosed. If your child has a diagnosis of autism spectrum disorder (the ICD-11's preferred term), ADHD or developmental language disorder, it is likely that the clinician will have been guided by the ICD-11's criteria for what constitutes each of those diagnostic labels.

Individual Education Plan (IEP) – This is a plan that will inform a school's work with a child, sharing the targets being worked on, the child's strengths, the child's current progress, the child's areas of difficulty and suggested classroom strategies to meet the child's needs. It is not required for a school to have IEPs for pupils, but it would be reasonable for a parent to ask a school how they communicate the things set out above with staff if they don't use IEPs. Some schools will have a similar document that they call a pupil passport or pupil profile.

Masking – Hiding or disguising parts of oneself in order to better fit in with those around you. This term is often used to describe the manner in which autistic people may work hard to follow social norms in public; this can be a cause of great stress for that person. For a school child, a day spent masking can result in more extreme dysregulated behaviour at home.

Neurodivergent – This is a term often used to describe people whose brains 'function in a different way to that usually considered as normal' (Collins, 2024a). In relation to SEND, children may be termed neurodivergent if they have a diagnosed condition such as ADHD, autism, dyslexia or dyspraxia.

Neurotypical – The Collins Dictionary describes neurotypical people as those who have 'brains that function in a way that is usually considered as normal' (Collins, 2024b), though I think many readers of this book would question the helpfulness of the concept of 'normal' here. It is a term often used to describe children and young people who are not on SEND registers.

Progress 8 – This describes the progress a pupil makes from the end of Key Stage 2 (KS2) (typically aged 11) until the end of KS4 (typically aged 16). As it is benchmarked against a child's individual KS2 score, a child can get below average GCSE grades but still have a positive Progress 8 score. A score of zero indicates the child making expected progress.

Reading age – It is common practice for schools to administer a reading test with their pupils. This is an important way for a school to understand your child's reading ability and to have a number against which they can measure progress. A school may contact you to say that your 14-year-old daughter has a reading age of eight years and six months, for example. See page 151 for more about the caution needed when looking at a reading age.

SEND Code of Practice – The statutory guidance that informs the work of educational settings in relation to children and young people with SEND.

SEND register – This is the term typically used by schools to describe their record of pupils who they consider to have a SEND.

SEN Support – Any child attending school with SEND, who doesn't have an EHCP, should be receiving what the school calls 'SEN Support'. For more information on what this might mean, see page 57.

Specialist Resource Provision – This is the term used when a school has been commissioned to provide specialist support within a mainstream setting. See page 87 for more details.

Standard Age Scores – Sometimes you'll see a score (on a school's reading test report, on a report written by a SEND professional such as an educational psychologist) called a 'SAS' or 'Standard Age Score'. This way of measuring a particular skill has 100 as the average. When you see scoring such as this, you can use the following to relate it to something that might be more meaningful to you, such as a percentage:

Standard Age Score	Percentile	Description
125	95	Superior
115	84	High average
100	50	Average
85	16	Low average
75	5	Below average

Summer born – For school admission purposes, 'summer born' refers to pupils born between 1 April and 31 August (Child Law Advice Service, 2023). See page 59 to learn where this is sometimes relevant in the context of SEND.

Synthetic phonics – An approach to learning to read that starts with the individual sounds within words (the 'phonemes') and maps them onto the letters that are commonly used to write them (the 'graphemes'). Children are taught to blend these individual sounds into words.

References

ADHD UK (2022) *ADHD Incidence*. https://adhduk.co.uk/adhd-incidence.

Blatchford, P., Bassett, P., Brown, P., Martin, C., Russell, A. and Webster, R. (2009) *Research Brief: Deployment and Impact of Support Staff Project. (Research Brief DCSF-RB1)*. London: Department for Children, Schools and Families.

British Dyslexia Association (2023a) *Dyscalculia*. www.bdadyslexia.org.uk/dyscalculia.

British Dyslexia Association (2023b) *Dyslexia*. www.bdadyslexia.org.uk/dyslexia.

Broderick, A. A. and Roscigno, R. (2021) 'Autism, inc.: the autism industrial complex.' *Journal of Disability Studies in Education 2*, 1, 77–101. https://doi.org/10.1163/25888803-bja10008.

Camden, B. (2015) 'Summer born pupils 90 per cent more likely to be on SEN register.' *Schools Week*, 6 March. www.bit.ly/3HIYfBy.

Child Law Advice Service (2023) *Summer Born Admission*. https://childlawadvice.org.uk/information-pages/summer-born-admissions.

Children and Families Act (2014). www.legislation.gov.uk/ukpga/2014/6/contents/enacted.

Children and Family Health Devon (n.d.) *Parents' Sleep Pack*. https://childrenandfamilyhealthdevon.nhs.uk/resources/developing-good-sleep-hygiene.

Children's Law Centre (2020). *What Is the SENDIST?* https://childrenslawcentre.org.uk/faqs/tag/sen/page/3.

Chronically Sick and Disabled Persons Act (1970). www.legislation.gov.uk/ukpga/1970/44.

Collins (2024a) 'Neurodivergent.' *Collins Dictionary*. www.collinsdictionary.com/dictionary/english/neurodivergent.

Collins (2024b) 'Neurotypical.' *Collins Dictionary*. www.collinsdictionary.com/dictionary/english/neurotypical.

Department for Education (2019) *Omnibus Survey of Pupils and Their Parents or Carers: Wave 6*. www.bit.ly/31jM5i3.

Department for Education (2023a) *Special and Educational Needs and Disability: An Analysis and Summary of Data Sources*. https://assets.publishing.service.gov.uk/media/64930eef103ca6001303a3a6/Special_educational_needs_and_disability_an_analysis_and_summary_of_data_sources.pdf.

Department for Education (2023b) *Special Educational Needs: Analysis and Summary of Data Sources*. www.gov.uk/government/publications/sen-analysis-and-summary-of-data-sources.

Department for Education (2023c) *SEND and Alternative Provision Improvement Plan*. www.gov.uk/government/publications/send-and-alternative-provision-improvement-plan.

Department for Education (2024a) *Transition to National Professional Qualification for Special Educational Needs Co-Ordinators*. www.gov.uk/government/publications/mandatory-qualification-for-sencos/transition-to-national-professional-qualification-for-special-educational-needs-co-ordinators.

Department for Education (2024b) *Special educational needs and disability: An analysis and summary of data sources*. https://assets.publishing.service.gov.uk/media/66bd-c2de3effd5b79ba490fd/Special_educational_needs_and_disability_analysis_and_summary_of_data_sources_Aug24.pdf.

Department for Education and Department of Health (2015) *SEND Code of Practice: 0 to 25 Years*. https://assets.publishing.service.gov.uk/media/5a7dcb85ed915d2ac884d995/SEND_Code_of_Practice_January_2015.pdf.

Department for Education and Skills (2003) *Data Collection by Type of Special Educational Need*. London: Department for Education and Skills.

Dyspraxia Foundation (2023) *Dyspraxia at a Glance*. https://dyspraxiafoundation.org.uk.

Education Endowment Foundation (2019) *Reciprocal Reading*. https://educationendowmentfoundation.org.uk/projects-and-evaluation/projects/reciprocal-reading.

Education Endowment Foundation (2021) *Working with Parents to Support Children's Learning*. https://educationendowmentfoundation.org.uk/education-evidence/guidance-reports/supporting-parents.

Education Endowment Foundation (n.d.) *High Quality Interactions in the Early Years: The 'ShREC' Approach*. https://d2tic4wvo1iusb.cloudfront.net/eef-guidance-reports/literacy-early-years/High_quality_interactions_in_the_Early_Years_-_The_'ShREC'_approach.pdf.

Equality Act (2010). www.legislation.gov.uk/ukpga/2010/15/contents.

Fletcher, D. and Sarkar, M. (2016) 'Mental fortitude training: An evidence-based approach to developing psychological resilience for sustained success.' *Journal of Sport Psychology in Action* 7, 3, 135–157.

Gorard, S. (2014) 'The link between academies in England, pupil outcomes and local patterns of socio-economic segregation between schools.' *Research Papers in Education* 29, 3, 268–284. https://doi.org/10.1080/02671522.2014.885726.

Great Ormond Street Hospital (GOSH) (2023) *Sleep Hygiene in Children and Young People*. www.gosh.nhs.uk/conditions-and-treatments/procedures-and-treatments/sleep-hygiene-children.

Gunderson, E. A., Gripshover, S. J., Romero, C., Dweck, C. S., Goldin⊠Meadow, S. and Levine, S. C. (2013) 'Parent praise to 1- to 3-year-olds predicts children's motivational frameworks 5 years later.' *Child Development* 84, 5, 1526–1541.

Hattersley, C. (2013) *Autism: Understanding Behaviour*. London: National Autistic Society.

HM Government (2022) *SEND Review: Right Support Right Place Right Time*. https://assets.publishing.service.gov.uk/media/624178c68fa8f5277c0168e7/SEND_review_right_support_right_place_right_time_accessible.pdf.

Holdsworth, S., Turner, M. and Scott-Young, C. M. (2018) '... Not drowning, waving. Resilience and university: A student perspective.' *Studies in Higher Education* 43, 11, 1837–1853.

IPSEA (n.d.(a)) *Asking for an EHC Needs Assessment*. www.ipsea.org.uk/asking-for-an-ehc-needs-assessment.

IPSEA (n.d.(b)) *How Your Nursery, School or College Should Help*. www.ipsea.org.uk/how-your-nursery-school-or-college-should-help#:~:text=The%20school%20can%20only%20exclude%20them%20from%20activities,other%20children%20or%20the%20efficient%20use%20of%20resources.

Jang, H. (2008) "Supporting students" motivation, engagement, and learning during an uninteresting activity.' *Journal of Educational Psychology 100*, 4, 798–811.

Lange, K. W., Reichl, S., Lange, K. M., Tucha, L. and Tucha, O. (2010) 'The history of attention deficit hyperactivity disorder.' *ADHD Attention Deficit and Hyperactivity Disorders 2*, 4, 241–255. https://doi.org/10.1007/s12402-010-0045-8.

Local Government Association (2023) *Local Area Special Educational Needs and Disabilities Report*. https://lginform.local.gov.uk/reports/view/send-research/local-area-send-report?mod-area=E06000031&mod-group=AllSingleTierAndCountyLaInCountry_England&mod-type=namedComparisonGroup.

McConnell, B. M. and Kubina, R. (2016) 'Parents using explicit reading instruction with their children at-risk for reading difficulties.' *Education and Treatment of Children 39*, 2, 115–140.

Ministry of Justice (2023). *Official Statistics: Tribunal Statistics Quarterly: July to September 2023*. www.gov.uk/government/statistics/tribunals-statistics-quarterly-july-to-september-2023/tribunal-statistics-quarterly-july-to-september-2023#annual-special-educational-needs-and-disability-send-statistics.

National Autistic Society (2023a) *What Is Autism?* www.autism.org.uk/advice-and-guidance/what-is-autism/the-history-of-autism.

National Autistic Society (2023b) *The History of Autism*. www.autism.org.uk/advice-and-guidance/what-is-autism/the-history-of-autism.

National Autistic Society (n.d.) *Demand Avoidance*. www.autism.org.uk/advice-and-guidance/topics/behaviour/demand-avoidance.

National Statistics (2023a) *Statistics: Special Educational Needs (SEN)*. www.gov.uk/government/collections/statistics-special-educational-needs-sen.

National Statistics (2023b) *Education, Health and Care Plans*. https://explore-education-statistics.service.gov.uk/find-statistics/education-health-and-care-plans.

National Statistics (2023c) *School Workforce in England*. https://explore-education-statistics.service.gov.uk/find-statistics/school-workforce-in-england.

National Statistics (2024) *Special Educational Needs in England, Academic Year 2023/24*. https://explore-education-statistics.service.gov.uk/find-statistics/special-educational-needs-in-england.

NHS (2021a) *Attention Deficit Hyperactivity Disorder (ADHD): Diagnosis*. www.nhs.uk/conditions/attention-deficit-hyperactivity-disorder-adhd/diagnosis.

NHS (2021b) *Attention Deficit Hyperactivity Disorder (ADHD): Symptoms*. www.nhs.uk/conditions/attention-deficit-hyperactivity-disorder-adhd/symptoms.

NHS (2023a) *Anxiety Disorders in Children*. www.nhs.uk/mental-health/children-and-young-adults/advice-for-parents/anxiety-disorders-in-children.

NHS (2023b) *Occupational Therapy*. www.nhs.uk/conditions/occupational-therapy.

NHS (n.d.). *Child Psychotherapy*. https://tavistockandportman.nhs.uk/visiting-us/treatments/child-psychotherapy.

NHS England (n.d.) *Making Information and the Words We Use Accessible*. www.england.nhs.uk/learning-disabilities/about/get-involved/involving-people/making-information-and-the-words-we-use-accessible.

NICE (2023) *Attention Deficit Hyperactivity Disorder: How Common Is It?* https://cks.nice. org.uk/topics/attention-deficit-hyperactivity-disorder/background-information/ prevalence.

Northern Ireland Statistics and Research Agency (2022) *Annual Enrolments at Schools and in Funded Pre-School Education in Northern Ireland 2021-22*. Bangor: Department of Education. https://www.education-ni.gov.uk/publications/annual-enrolments-schools-and-funded-pre-school-education-northern-ireland-2021-22.

Pye, S. (2020) 'Marmalade Chunks.' *There She Goes*, Series 2, Episode 5. London: BBC Two: 6 August 2020.

Rattan, A., Good, C. and Dweck, C. (2012) 'It's ok—Not everyone can be good at math: instructors with an entity theory comfort (and demotivate) students.' *Journal of Experimental Social Psychology 48*, 3, 731–737.

Rosenthal, R. and Jacobson, L. (1966) 'Teachers' expectancies: Determinants of pupils' IQ gains.' *Psychological Reports 19*, 1, 115–118. https://doi.org/10.2466/pr0.1966.19.1.115.

Royal College of Speech and Language Therapists. (n.d.) *What Is Speech and Language Therapy?* www.rcslt.org/wp-content/uploads/media/Project/RCSLT/rcslt-what-is-slt-factsheet.pdf.

Russell, G., Stapley, S., Newlove-Delgado, T., Salmon, A., *et al.* (2022). 'Time trends in autism diagnosis over 20 years: A UK population-based cohort study.' *Journal of Child Psychology and Psychiatry, and Allied Disciplines 63*, 6, 674–682. https://doi.org/10.1111/jcpp.13505.

Sala, R., Amet, L., Blagojevic-Stokic, N., Shattock, P. and Whiteley, P. (2020). 'Bridging the gap between physical health and autism spectrum disorder.' *Neuropsychiatric Disease and Treatment, 16*, 1605–1618. https://doi.org/10.2147/NDT.S251394.

Scottish Government (2022) *Schools in Scotland 2022: Summary Statistics*. www.gov. scot/publications/summary-statistics-for-schools-in-scotland-2022/pages/classes-and-pupils.

The Special Educational Needs and Disability Regulations (2014). www.legislation. gov.uk/uksi/2014/1530/contents/made.

The Warnock Report (1978) *Report of the Committee of Enquiry into the Education of Handicapped Children and Young People*. London: Her Majesty's Stationery Office. https://education-uk.org/documents/warnock/warnock1978.html.

Tirraoro, T. (2023a) '84% of Ombudsman Complaints about Education and Children's Services Upheld.' *Special Needs Jungle*. www.specialneedsjungle. com/84-ombudsman-complaints-education-childrens-services-upheld.

Tirraoro, T. (2023b) 'The Government's SEND Improvement Plan: An Initial Overview.' *Special Needs Jungle*. www.specialneedsjungle.com/the-governments-send-improvement-plan-an-initial-overview.

Tolstoy, L. (2016) *Anna Karenina*. Translated by R. Bartlett. Oxford: Oxford University Press.

Truman, C. (2021). *The Teacher's Introduction to Pathological Demand Avoidance: Practical Strategies for the Classroom*. London: Jessica Kingsley Publishers.

UK Government (n.d.(a)) *Employers: Preventing Discrimination*. www.gov.uk/employer-preventing-discrimination.

UK Government (n.d.(b)) *Access to Work: Get Support If You Have a Disability or Health Condition*. www.gov.uk/access-to-work.

UK Government (n.d.(c)) *Disability Living Allowance (DLA) for children: Eligibility*. www. gov.uk/disability-living-allowance-children/eligibility.

UK Parliament (2023) *Special Educational Needs: Finance: Question for Department for Education UIN 5684, Tabled on 6 December 2023*. https://questions-statements.parliament.uk/written-questions/detail/2023-12-06/5684.

United Nations (1994) *The Salamanca Statement and Framework for Action on Special Needs Education*. https://unesdoc.unesco.org/ark:/48223/pf0000098427.

Welsh Government (2023) *Schools' Census Results (Headline Statistics): January 2023*. www.gov.wales/schools-census-results-headline-statistics-january-2023.

Whitehurst, G. J. and Lonigan, C. J. (1998) 'Child development and emergent literacy.' *Child Development 69*, 3, 848–872.

World Health Organization (2021) *Deafness and Hearing Loss*. www.who.int/news-room/fact-sheets/detail/deafness-and-hearing-loss.

World Health Organization (2022) *ICD-11 for Mortality and Morbidity Statistics*. Geneva: WHO. https://icd.who.int/browse11/l-m/en.

Young Minds (2022) *Strategies You Can Try at Home*. www.youngminds.org.uk/parent/parents-a-z-mental-health-guide/school-anxiety-and-refusal/#Strategiesyoucantryathome.

Young Minds (n.d.) *School Anxiety and Refusal: Parent Guide to Support*. www.youngminds.org.uk/parent/parents-a-z-mental-health-guide/school-anxiety-and-refusal.

Bibliography

American Psychiatric Association (2013) *Diagnostic and Statistical Manual of Mental Disorders, Fifth Edition.* https://dsm.psychiatryonline.org/doi/book/10.1176/appi.books.9780890425596.

Aubin, G. (2022) *The Lone SENDCO.* Woodbridge: John Catt.

Baron-Cohen, S. (2008) *Autism and Asperger Syndrome.* Oxford: Oxford University Press.

Davis, E. (2021) 'Pre-phonics is the key to early reading.' *Famly.* www.famly.co/blog/prephonics-early-reading.

Donvan, J. and Zucker, C. (2016) *In a Different Key.* London: Penguin.

Dowling, C., Nicoll, N. and Thomas, B. (2006) *A Different Kind of Perfect: Writings by Parents on Raising a Child with Special Needs.* Boulder, CO: Shambhala Publications.

Durrant, G. (2021) *100 Ways Your Child Can Learn Through Play.* London: Jessica Kingsley Publishers.

Fleming, E. and MacAlister, L. (2016) *Toilet Training and the Autism Spectrum (ASD).* London: Jessica Kingsley Publishers.

Gray, C. (2002) *My Social Stories Book.* London: Jessica Kingsley Publishers.

Jorgensen, R. G. (2023) *Supporting Your Child with Special Needs: 50 Fundamental Tools for Families.* New York: Routledge.

Kirkpatrick, A. (2008) *Pyschovertical.* London: Hutchinson.

Lancy, D. (2017) *Raising Children: Surprising Insights from Other Cultures.* Cambridge: Cambridge University Press.

Liedloff, J. (1975) *The Continuum Concept.* London: Duckworth.

Ministry of Justice (2022) *Tribunal Statistics Quarterly: July to September 2022.* www.gov.uk/government/statistics/tribunal-statistics-quarterly-july-to-september-2022/tribunal-statistics-quarterly-july-to-september-2022.

National Statistics (2023a) *Education, Health and Care Plans: Reporting Year 2023.* https://explore-education-statistics.service.gov.uk/find-statistics/education-health-and-care-plans#dataBlock-1b7eaac0-575d-4a36-b46f-fd54d20ade58-tables.

National Statistics (2023b) *Special Educational Needs in England, Academic Year 2022/23.* https://explore-education-statistics.service.gov.uk/find-statistics/special-educational-needs-in-england#dataBlock-b8855149-2ceb-41e7-81c6-9ea253f9c86d-tables.

Solomon, A. (2012) *Far from the Tree: Parents, Children and the Search for Identity.* New York: Scribner.

UK Government (n.d.) *Disability Living Allowance (DLA) for Children*. www.gov.uk/
disability-living-allowance-children.
Wing, L. (1996) *The Autistic Spectrum*. London: Robinson.

Appendix

Example of a Toilet Plan
Jamie's Toilet Plan[1]

HISTORY

Jamie is four years old and is autistic. His parents tried to 'potty train' at age two – with no success – using standard approaches.

CURRENT SITUATION AND READINESS

Jamie understands some spoken language if it is clear and familiar. He is comfortable with visual communication including symbols. He has some mild motor difficulties including difficulty with coordination and body awareness. Despite this, he is interested in the toilet and observing toileting and he does have a basic awareness of body functions and himself in relation to them.

Jamie wears nappies day and night and has done since birth. He sometimes shows some awareness of needing to go but most of the time he does not. Overall, he is still learning the necessary physical cues needed for toilet independence. He needs the toilet at regular times through the day and there is no discernible pattern or timetable.

He has some resistance to sitting on a potty or toilet and generally will not do so when asked. However, visual cues have worked for other self-care routines, so these may lessen his anxiety around the toilet. More physical support (e.g., a more supporting seat) might prove to be useful.

Jamie has some sensory issues related to toileting. For example,

---

1   'Jamie' is a fictional child.

he dislikes dry toilet paper and only likes wet baby wipes. He generally dislikes being touched.

Jamie responds really well to routine, and we anticipate that if toilet time were an established part of his visual timetable, he would respect this.

All in all, Jamie is most likely ready to learn more around toileting in a supported and consistent programme. He has learnt other self-care routines successfully with support.

TOILET TARGETS

1. To begin a consistent routine of sitting on the toilet as soon as possible.
2. To gradually learn to use the toilet and to reduce reliance on nappies.
3. To cease using nappies but continue with adult support.
4. To be fully independent when he's ready.

TOILET TEAM

- Parents
- School – key worker, teacher, SENDCO and other support staff
- Local authority autism outreach team – consultation/advice

JAMIE'S PREFERRED/FAMILIAR VOCABULARY

- Pee
- Poo
- Nappy
- Wipes
- Toilet
- Potty
- Willy
- Bum bum

TOILET PLAN
Phase 0 (already in progress)

- Desensitize Jamie to toileting with an 'open door' policy at home and talking about toileting openly and without stigma or pressure.
- Change Jamie's nappies in the bathroom and always flush poo away down the toilet with Jamie observing.
- Offer Jamie the toilet if he indicates a need.

Phase 1 (to begin as soon as possible)

- Hold a 'toilet team' briefing to agree the plan.
- Introduce a social story about using the toilet and read this to Jamie regularly but without any expected action in the moment.
- Display toileting sequence symbols at home (and ensure they match school).
- Review Phase 1 after two weeks.

Phase 2

- Introduce a toilet time symbol on Jamie's visual timetable and follow the visual toileting sequence with Jamie, asking him to sit for increasing amounts of time (start with, e.g., 30 seconds, leading up to three minutes) using a timer.
- Reward any wees or poos on the toilet with celebratory verbal praise, but otherwise have a low-pressure/-expectation approach.
- Gradually increase the number of visits to the toilet through the day.
- Review Phase 2 and plan next steps after three months.